A Time for India
2nd Edition

Dan Ellens and
Lakshmi Srinivas

Dan Ellens has written several books, including:

Turning Ten – Great Adventures in the Great Lakes
2nd Edition

Building the Bunkee – A Photo Anthology of Custom Log
Cabin Construction and One Man's Retirement Dream

Treehouse Letters
The Unabridged Michigan Forest Life Journal

Visit Ellens' author profile page at BookBaby Publishing

https://store.bookbaby.com/profile/Dan_Ellens

First Edition
Copyright © 2006 by Daniel S. Ellens
ISBN 0-533-15092-2
Published by Vantage Press, Inc

Second Edition
Copyright @ 2023 by Daniel S. Ellens
BookBaby Publishing

Printed in the USA
ISBN 978-1-66789-174-3

Dan:
For Cathy,
the person with whom I share these memories.

Lakshmi:
For my parents and grandparents,
who have made me what I am.
For Srinivas and his parents,
who have taken me for what I am.

Contents

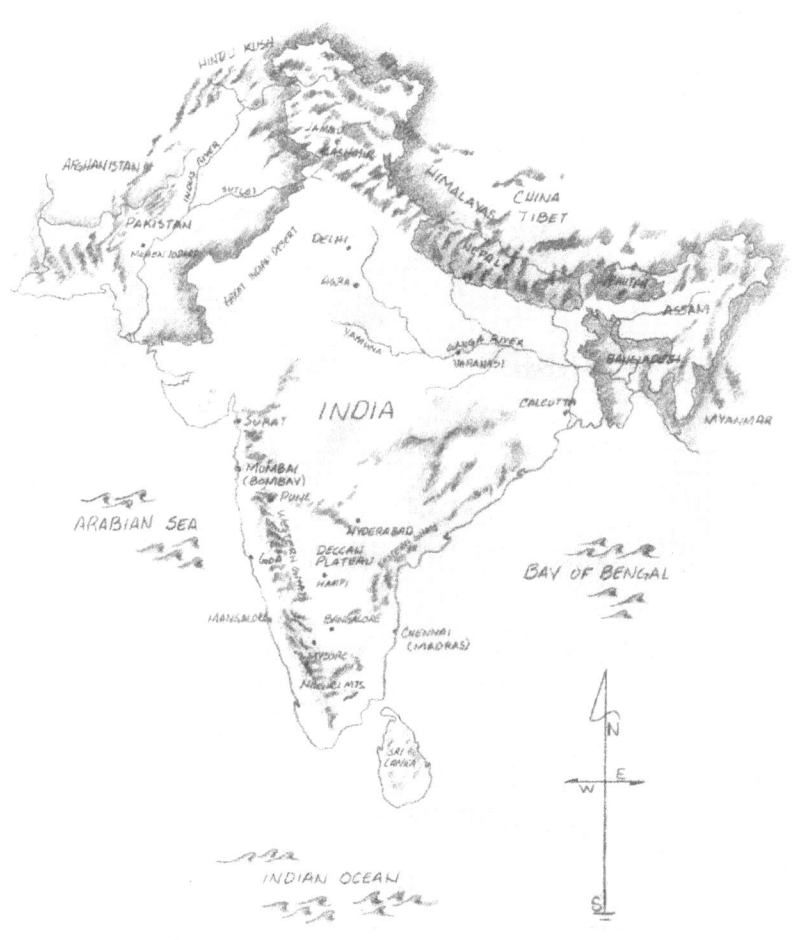

Preface

I have often wished I had been born in a different time: a time when society was less mature, when small changes could have large impacts. I thought with awe of my father's father, who lived from 1903 until 1996, the 20th century, nearly from beginning to end. He lived before electricity was common, before radio and television, before air travel and space travel, before boxed cake mixes. He lived much of his life at a time a twelve-mile journey from McBain to Cadillac, Michigan was an all-day outing. It was a time when resourcefulness was essential to survival, when living required more than having a job, and when life itself was well beyond the grasp of ordinary health care.

To make matters more interesting, my grandfather's world was the woods of northern Michigan at a time when technology in that part of the country lagged far behind what the rest of America had to offer. I was envious of the control my grandfather had over his existence. I liked the direct way his actions influenced his life, and the way that living was not merely a degree of the quality of life but rather a matter of life and death. Every action reflected on his own daily life and the life of his family. He could draw a breath of the crisp winter air knowing that if he finished watering the cattle in the subzero temperatures, they would be alive to milk the next day.

When I took an assignment in India in July 1996, my family of six traveled through time. We left mainstream America and entered into a world that was not only culturally different from the middle-class suburban society to which we were accustomed, but also in many ways more primitive than our life. India was a land of acute contrast and a land in the midst of massive change. For India, this was a time of industrial revolution, transforming major components of infrastructure, industry, and society from 1903 to 1996 in one giant step. During our stay, I often thought about my grandfather's life and felt like we were given a small chance to see life through his eyes. We lived with one foot in each time period and experienced something that is rare for most Americans.

There were times when we felt so cut off from our homeland that we might as well have been on the moon. It reminded me of an essay written by my mother's aunt, who, as a child, traveled by covered wagon with my mother's father deep into the uncharted American Southwest, homesteading in a place now known as Lewis, Colorado. She wrote that they "traveled into space." They went into a place that was unknown and mysterious, cut off from the past. They were pioneers, expanding America's frontier for future generations.

It was with the same loneliness and uncertainty that we left our comfortable surroundings for a different life in India. The challenge of confronting and conquering these doubts drew us to this *new* old world. We knew that we could not undertake such an endeavor without being better off for having done it. We hoped that in the end, we would find a satisfaction that ordinary life in Michigan could not generate.

Each evening during our stay, my wife, Cathy, the children, and I would sit at the dinner table and talk about what we had encountered that day. With our American perspective, it was difficult to leave the table without a good chuckle about something. Sometimes the situations were comical to us because of their absurdly extreme inefficiencies. Sometimes they were comical because of our cultural differences. Sometimes they were comical because of the surprise we found in their obvious and ingenious simplicity. And sometimes they were comical because of their tragic and seemingly avoidable circumstances. It is from these dinner-table discussions that this book evolved. The humor in the book is offered with respect and a heartfelt love for the country of India and the people whom we knew during our stay.

No experience in India can be truly understood without a historical and cultural context. For those who have not had the chance to grow up in India or live in the Indian culture, alternating chapters have been included in this text to provide that historical and cultural summary—what makes India what it is today. I am exceedingly grateful to Lakshmi Srinivas, presently a resident of Bangalore, who spent much of her life growing up in Chennai, for contributing some of the chapters herein.

About the Geography
by Lakshmi Srinivas

Like many countries of the world, India has her share of lofty mountains, valleys, passes, hills, rivers, seas, forests, islands, and beaches. Historical monuments, geographical wonders, and tourist locations that are scattered across the land provoke thoughts of what made up India's past and how India has become what it is today.

The geography of a country has a profound impact on its history. Climate, a factor of geography, influences civilization—the character of the people, their life, and activities. Professions adopted by inhabitants; the types of industries and the nature of trade; travel routes of merchants; pilgrims and armies; customs and traditions; social and political systems; and interaction with people of neighboring lands—all are greatly influenced by geographical features.

India is a peninsula with the Himalayas forming a nearly invincible barrier in the north. During the Middle Ages, the Himalayas separated the subcontinent, which was then comprised of present-day India, Pakistan, Bangladesh, and Bhutan, from the rest of Asia. Medieval invaders who did find a way to enter India through the northern mountain passes found few physical barriers to check their further advance. The rugged Himalayas lead to plains, stretching nearly 3000 kilometers west to east, watered by three great river systems: the Indus, the Ganges, and the Brahmaputra. India's fertile northern plains were an attractive destination for foreign invaders.

In the south, the Eastern and Western Ghats are mountain ranges bordering the shorelines of the Indian peninsula. These mountains form the boundaries of the Deccan plateau in the south.

The western coast of India, in some regions called the Konkan coast and in others called the Malabar coast, spans from Kutch in Gujarat to Kanyakumari in Tamil Nadu and is washed by the Arabian sea. The eastern coast, called the Coromandel coast, borders the Bay of Bengal. Kanyakumari, also known as Cape Comorin, is the southernmost tip of the country, a spot where the Indian Ocean, the Bay of Bengal, and the Arabian Sea meet. Islands of India that dot the seas are the Andaman and Nicobar Islands of the Bay of Bengal, and Amindivi, Lakshadweep, and Minicoy of the Arabian Sea.

Since India gained her independence, political boundaries of the subcontinent have changed. In 1947 Pakistan emerged as a separate country, divided into

East Pakistan and West Pakistan. In 1971 East Pakistan, which had been set aside from the Bengal province of India, became the independent country of Bangladesh.

Today India has a total of twenty-eight states, including three new states added in 2001—Jharkhand, Uttaranchal and Chattisgarh, carved out of Bihar, Uttar Pradesh, and Madhya Pradesh.

Acknowledgments

I have had the good fortune to work in an environment where my personal strengths and aspirations have been supported by my colleagues. I would like to thank Brian Stewart and George Webb, who believed that developing an enterprise in India to support India's own industrial growth was commercially viable, for entrusting that assignment to me, and for supporting my family during our stay.

I would like to extend my appreciation to Gautam Nevatia, a business partner who has become a true friend; to M.G. Pramod, who helped Cathy and me to better understand India; to Selvan, our devoted driver; and to the entire team of engineers and business associates in India whose work made our efforts worthwhile. We could not have done without their support, and they will remain in our memories forever.

The events described in the first edition of this book took place between 1996 and 1998. During that time, numerous people contributed in many ways to our experience in India and to bringing the first edition to print. My gratitude to those individuals has been acknowledged in the original book.

Finally, I would like to thank Lakshmi Srinivas for her insightful help in understanding change that has taken place in India since 2006 when the first edition was completed, and for her willingness to rewrite Chapter 14, "India Today", bringing the chapter up to date with India in 2023.

2023 Observations
The Passage of Time

"For some, there is fear that India is moving too fast, for others, not fast enough."

—Ayaz Memon and Ranjona Banerji
from *India 50 - The Making of a Nation*

Nearly twenty years ago, when I originally selected the title for this book, *A Time for India*, I sensed that India and the world were experiencing one swing in the perpetual movement of a global pendulum—something that would slowly approach an apex, and then, with a predictable kind of cultural, political, and economic inertia fed by all the forces of human nature, retreat to a new home position while slowly building up energy to begin another swing. Each swing measured in decades. Each swing moving India closer to levels of technology and infrastructure common in much of the rest of the world. India had plenty of catching up to do.

As a new age built on a vast and colorful history, trends were emerging in India that my own mind imagined as two expanding graphs. The first with one line following the world's changing appetite for globalization, intersecting with a second line indicating India's willingness to provide services outside of its borders. Another graph was laying out a line reflecting India's desire to achieve social infrastructure on par with other countries in Asia, Europe, and North America, alongside a line showing India's interest and ability to rebuild itself from within. The period about which the book was originally written (1996-1998) was the beginning of India's modern industrial revolution which fueled increased mobility for Indians at all levels of the social structure, broader access to communication, a wider exposure to information, and easier access to a large selection of new things that the rest of the world had already enjoyed for some time. That time, the time of my assignment in India, seemed to be near the starting point on both graphs when the lines began to change from static level positions to trajectories that showed plenty of movement.

Since my assignment, I have returned to India more than 80 times, each time enduring the difficulties and benefits of change underway. Each time marveling at the rapid rate at which change was taking place. And, yes, despite India's inherent chaos, the complete package of change—transportation, communication, public utilities, banking, and commerce—seemed to be following a logical plan with one step leading to the next. My Indian colleagues who lived the change from day to day, perhaps only seeing the chaos, often remarked about how slowly and inefficiently it was all occurring, almost at an imperceptible rate. But my own eyes saw it differently. Brief snapshots every few months made it easy for me to watch India's remarkably large, continuous strides with a kind of outsider's view. When reflecting back to the time of my assignment, and understanding the monumental mountain of red tape that must have been waded through to complete even the smallest steps of India's city projects, I stood in awe.

I think back to a small greenfield factory we built in a new industrial area on the outskirts of Bangalore in the early 2000s. The sloped terrain on this five-acre rock parcel was leveled in order to comply with *vastu* recommendations and to prepare an even surface for its building. A small team of subcontracted workers lived on site and completed the task using dynamite, a small, ordinary Mahindra utility tractor, and a heavy-duty, two-wheeled, wood-sided trailer. Based on all the options available in those days, this local solution did not seem so outdated or impractical. What really took time, though, was the municipality who was responsible for bringing in electricity needed to operate the factory. I do not know why this was an ongoing surprise. Ours was the first plot to be developed in a three-phase industrial complex. Nothing was delivered by the municipality within the timeframe they had promised. It was not even close. Not only the industrial area's electricity and water infrastructure lagged but so did the red-tape-ladened permits required for each step.

As we completed the factory's construction and its related office structure, we eventually brought in and restored second-hand European factory machinery to like-new condition. Our project was already nine months behind schedule. For construction like this, delay was more common than not, and not many people were seriously worried, perhaps because they felt helpless in the face of uncontrollable circumstances. But the developing financial problem was also not so hard to see. Carrying the loan we had drawn on to finance the construction while delaying production and revenue expected from sold-product for months built up quite a bit of unplanned interest cost. Indian annual interest rates were 12%–18% at the time. To keep the project from falling into a financial abyss, we reached into our pockets and ran our own utility poles for several kilometers from the nearest power station to the factory. We also bored our own water well. The project went on-line one year late and took five years to catch up to and overtake its original financial projections.

So, building a new network of second-level roads (affectionately called flyovers) crisscrossing the tightly congested city of Bangalore, while at the same time relocating segments of the population, lopping off pieces of homes, installing urban utility systems, training people to operate India's first cement-mixing trucks, and managing the daily chaos of Indian traffic seemed like something only God could do. I stood in awe.

When stepping off an airplane that has landed in one of India's new international airports, it is easy to overlook some of the hidden-from-view upgrades that are now part of Indian life, and to simply accept the benefits while imagining that life was always this good. The fiber optic communication cable that is now embedded below ground along every major roadside, which enables high-speed digital communication. The electric grid that seems to work steadily, despite exponentially increasing power usage. Perhaps today's electrical output is due to full reservoirs behind India's hydroelectric dams, a factor that varies from year to year. Perhaps it is due to India's new wind farms with acres of modern wind turbines lined up in neat rows. Perhaps it is due to the solar panels, installed by municipalities and private companies alike in a country that never seems to lack sun.

It is easy to not see the upgrades to India's banking infrastructure, though visitors who were last on the subcontinent in 1996 will immediately be surprised by the modern mechanisms for transactions at all levels of society. India has moved in nearly imperceptible steps from cash transactions and bank drafts with long queues at disconnected banks, to ATMs handing out small sums of cash, and finally to cashless pay apps on smartphones. But to make each of these improvements practical, India first needed to shift to a more reliable electric infrastructure. At the same time, India moved from its sparsely available private telephone land lines (which took years on a waiting list for ordinary citizens to acquire and which were supplemented by dark public telephone kiosks staffed around-the-clock by sandal-footed attendants who sat in shady spots within each kiosk) to simple first-generation private cell phones (whose ownership was highly regulated), and then to the modern smartphones available in one day to almost anyone in India and set up with data plans that most people could afford. Even to find smartphone inventory available with nearly every supplier every day across India is a marvel that travelers are unlikely to notice.

It is factors such as these that continue to drive the image of India still today as a land of remarkable contrast. Because now, a fruit seller pushing a colorful, wooden-wheeled cart to a favorite spot in the shade of a mighty banyan tree will bargain with customers wanting bananas or mangos and complete the transaction using a smartphone pay app enabled by a QR code mounted to the side of the cart.

Or consider the auto-rickshaw driver who still weaves unpredictably from one lane to the next but now follows GPS directions on a smartphone mounted to the tiny dashboard of his vehicle. Well, that is interesting. Because of India's heritage for unlabeled turns, one-way alleys, and shortcuts, the driver - whose mother-tongue is almost certainly the local language - might hear a voice in distinctive American accent coming from the smartphone GPS, literally instructing him to turn left after the second pillar supporting an overpass. The autorickshaw itself is no longer the animal it used to be. The days of pull-start gasoline engines have given way to LPG fuel and electric-start. Horns are now electric, rather than old-school coiled brass funnels with their squeeze-bulb ends. And a new electric single windshield wiper has replaced the hand-operated one of years gone by.

While the autorickshaw, with its three-wheeled charm, has from the beginning been part of India's transportation evolution (perhaps transportation revolution), contrasting traffic partners have moved the autorickshaw a few steps lower on the hierarchy of the road. One will see the world's most luxurious sedans, electric vehicles, a full range of trucks - old and new - motor scooters and motorcycles of all types. Now, there is rarely a bicycle. And in the countryside during the time of harvest, one will certainly still see wooden-wheeled carts filled with sugar cane pulled by two white bulls with bells on the ends of their horns.

A few years after Bangalore's main thoroughfares were divided at their centers with stone, curb-like barriers, after modern expressways were built to skirt the outer edges of the whole metropolis connecting nearby villages as they grew, after the first phase of the elevated monorail

—the Metro—was added between two busy parts of the city, and at about the same time that the second-level flyovers saw their first traffic, a new character fell upon Bangalore. It all seemed an impossibility. City streets that had always been considered a precarious form of two-way traffic were converted to single direction use. Traffic signals were added. Lane discipline was suggested. Land was taken for road expansion projects, often cutting existing homes or shops down the middle, leaving open rooms exposed in full view until construction in the area was completed and the dust had settled. Homes that bordered the new second-level routes found a noisy symphony of vehicles racing by their second-story windows with their doors and balconies shaded by a ribbon of elevated highway rather than a balmy tunnel of flowering trees. New drain systems and other utilities were installed with the roads.

When a new road project was finally finished, the traffic it carried had already grown so dramatically that the new path immediately needed to be doubled in size again. As shopping malls, high-rise apartments, and glass-clad office buildings popped up, provisions were also added for maze-like, multi-level parking structures. Farms and open range that had surrounded the city were converted to neighborhoods, industrial complexes, and golf courses. The city has never stopped growing. While old Bangalore began to disappear like an ancient temple being absorbed into a jungle—in this case, a jungle of modern city structures—the city's name was nostalgically returned to its pre-British indigenous label for the original village: Bengaluru.

Today, people visiting Bengaluru, a city with a 2022 population of 13.2 million (up from a 1996 population of 4.9 million), will find traffic-filled, multi-laned, multi-level highways connecting many neighborhoods. A visitor is likely to arrive at an organized, world-class, modern international airport, with nearly 30 kilometers of manicured, garden-lined highway between the airport and the city center. The city has tried to mute the stereotypic first impression of visitors to India who have traditionally returned home after their adventure on the subcontinent with stories of the intense chaos of India's high-volume humanity, unmanaged debris filling every ditch, loose cattle sharing the streets, and stray dogs wandering from doorstep to doorstep. This new first impression—today's park-like setting on arrival—is short-lived for those who venture further than India's five-star hotels and upscale dining venues. Those who step onto a nearby sidewalk and walk into a neighborhood will find a city alive with growth, noise, and movement. It will be filled with heat bubbling up from the environment and the humanity that inhabits it.

Now, McDonald's and Burger King compete within sight of each other for fast food customers with India's own brand of the drive-through window, which may be more suitable for a two-wheeled scooter than a full-size sedan. Air-conditioned, multi-level shopping malls are scattered about the city. Commercial Street and its surrounding shopping district includes a combination of 21st century, glass-fronted venues, and small, one-person, wooden-shuttered stalls that close briefly during each call to prayer. Hindu temples and Muslim mosques shoehorned between neighborhood buildings, old and new, each broadcast their own style of spiritual music into a street already filled with other sounds of the city.

Bengaluru's rapid growth is only one part of the general migration from rural India to its cities that has marked India's last 25 years. Much of this may be another generation of maturing children who imagine greener pastures in busy metropolises. Exciting and adventuresome. Desires and decisions of India's people, urban or rural, educated or illiterate, are now fueled by easily accessible information about a broader world which they did not see one generation ago and which now confronts them digitally on smartphones.

The urban draw of undergraduate and post-graduate education entices rural students with now more than 1,000 Indian universities competing for a new cohort of students each year. Employment opportunities for graduates are most often found in India's populated urban centers where infrastructure exists to support India's businesses. Indian manufacturing companies, each occupying a position in an industrial supply stream, are also most often set up in areas at the outskirts of India's cities where support infrastructure exists. These enterprises attract both skilled and unskilled labor, many of whom come from rural agricultural settings in India's countryside.

One of the most invisible factors changing within India is the continuous pressure applied by the Indian companies that truly embrace robust quality improvement processes within their own businesses and supply streams. It touches every sector. It is a journey without end. Organizations embracing this attitude have participated in the advancement of India in an interconnected way.

Perhaps the medical sector is a good illustration. In 1996, we arrived in India with very little available as a local medical safety net. The entire medical sector was frightening to us with few systematic processes that could be depended on. Today, a network of modern, private, world-class hospitals is sprinkled around India. Reliable power, clean water, and internet communication make these hospitals possible. For more than a decade, the domestic activity of these facilities has been an underlying foundation for a small medical tourism industry that performs complex procedures for foreigners seeking moderately-priced, high-quality care. Despite brick-and-mortar infrastructure achievements, this segment could not have emerged or have sustained its presence without dependable quality processes at the forefront of each hospital's operations.

As a portion of companies throughout all Indian sectors focus more intently on the science of quality improvement, an old theme that haunted everything done in India during 1996, seems to be slowly vanishing. A neighbor who lived in our Bengaluru apartment complex used the saying, "Directly from the construction to the repair phase." It made us chuckle. Today, some of that is disappearing. Perhaps one more generation of change, permeating the most basic thinking of all those inhabiting the subcontinent, will lead to the irrelevance of this comical observation. And as things like this subtly evaporate from the landscape, it is good to know that a traveler can still arrive in India setting one foot in the century of today and the other in a century of 200 years ago. They will not escape the experience without facing the contrast, mystery, and magic of a land exploding with heritage and potential. What they find in India will have as much to do with themselves as it has to do with the land and people of India.

1

Meeting Ravi

"The area we know as India is nearly half as large as the United States. Its population is three times greater than ours. Its import and export trade - as yet but a germ of the possible - amounted, in the year 1924-25 to about two and a half billion dollars. And Bombay is but three weeks' journey from New York."

—Katherine Mayo, 1927,
from *Mother India*

It was a hot day early in July when we arrived in Bangalore after nearly two days of air travel, waiting lounges, and great anticipation. The damp, musty smell of Indian air greeted us as we walked down the metal steps from the plane onto the tarmac, following a trail of other passengers across the handmade pavement and through the unmarked arrival door of the terminal. A stream of working ladies navigated a piece of rough timber with baskets of dirt on their heads as they climbed out of a deep pit in the ground. In the pit, men worked with hooked shovels digging and filling the baskets in an endless chain of activities that would in time result in a footing for the new terminal that was under construction.

This was the day that we met M. G. Pramod—or Pammi, as we came affectionately to know him. From across the arrivals hall, Pammi's jovial smile connected with our expressions of relief, and a long relationship began with the man who would take us by the hand and eliminate every barrier we could not conquer on our own during our stay in this foreign land.

Even before our arrival, Pammi had considered many hotel options in the city, and in an effort to ensure that we were well looked after, had made arrangements at one of Bangalore's oldest and finest—the Windsor Manor. The hotel had one of the few three-room suites available in the region. It was a setting that could comfortably accommodate two adults and four children.

Pammi had also arranged for a car and driver to be temporarily available to us until we could acquire our own vehicle. The car had a license plate attached to the rear bumper displaying in bold characters the number 3777. Pammi explained that the car should be asked for at the hotel, restaurants, or other places by using this number. Before dismissing the driver on the first afternoon, I asked him to be sure to return the following morning. We intended to start the children in their new school immediately and had a schedule to keep. I asked for his name.

"Ravi, sir," he answered.

When we walked into the hotel, a manager with a neatly-pressed dark suit and flawless manners introduced himself. It was his intention to extend every hospitality during our stay. Handing me his calling card, he volunteered to sort out any problems we encountered. We stepped into the elevator. I pulled the card from my shirt pocket. His name was also Ravi.

Early the next morning we returned to the lobby to find the welcoming smile and outstretched hand of manager Ravi. He called for car 3777. A vaguely familiar white Contessa soon appeared under the entry canopy. We recognized the car, but something didn't seem quite the same about the driver. Using Kannada, the local language of the Bangalore region, the concierge gave the driver instructions to deliver us to the children's school in Yelahanka.

As we traveled along roads we had never seen before to a location we knew little about, we sensed something strange about the driver. He was the same size as the driver we expected. He looked nearly the same. His English was about the same. Yet there was a subtle difference not easy to identify. The route continued to wind through narrow back roads of Bangalore, and his eyes were visible in the mirror. After nearly 15 kilometers Cathy and I were both convinced that the person behind the wheel was not our original driver. Leaning over the seat, Cathy asked for his name.

"Ravi, madam," he replied.

Interesting. Maybe we were mistaken.

Entering the office that morning, Pammi was waiting for me. He had some initial formalities that needed to be addressed. First, we needed to run copies of our passports and visas in order to apply for residency in India. Pammi called the office boy.

Pammi explained, "This man will take your passports and do the needful. His name is Ravi."

I hid my surprise. Pammi proceeded to introduce the people in the office. He began with the senior man in purchasing.

"This is the man who will look after getting your belongings cleared through customs. His name is Ravi."

I questioned my sanity. The next person was Soni, a woman who had been assigned as my secretary. Soni was a name that seemed easy to remember, until Suma the woman at the reception desk was introduced. Soni and Suma—keeping this straight would be a challenge. I asked Soni to contact an individual at the accounting firm who was to help with setting up a bank account and reached into my briefcase to find the written instructions given to me in Michigan several weeks earlier. The contact for the accounting firm was underlined—*Ravi.*

Cathy would need to hear about this in the evening. It seemed incredible. On one hand, it would be easy to remember the name of almost everyone we had met. On the other hand, could there be any way to keep this information straight; Ravi the first, Ravi the second— like the kings of England? This was very strange. How many men in Bangalore were *not* named Ravi?

Later that day Cathy and I went to visit the accounting firm with Ravi to start the endless stream of paperwork for the Indian government. The office was on the 14th floor of Mittal Towers, one of Bangalore's tallest buildings. As we stood waiting for the elevator to reach the ground floor, we noticed a paper posted prominently on the wall.

"All tenants are responsible for putting mesh over windows and vent openings since monkeys have been entering the building and turning on water taps and wreaking havoc with electronic equipment."

Which was the more serious offense, using the washrooms or operating the computers?

During the next few days, our lives were inundated with all the experiences that newcomers would notice. There was never a time that at least one of the six of us was not sick. Another hotel guest labeled our most common ailment *Delhi belly,* something we never really got rid of during our stay in India, but that we eventually didn't even notice we still had.

Our suite was on the hotel's top floor. The Windsor Manor was an elegant hotel, constructed and managed in the British tradition. From our window we could see the roofs of the city and flocks of light green parrots flying about the treetops. On the third morning the children found a lizard scaling the mirror in their bathroom. They captured it and brought it to the floor manager, asking him to release it outside, since they were in their pajamas. The manager showed great interest in this lizard, trying to make the children feel important. The lizard was a nice find, and even a bit of a cute creature. It seemed a bit unusual to us coming from Michigan, where lizards are found mainly in zoos. I had no idea that it would be only a matter of weeks until we would be chasing these critters with a vengeance (and a broom) through our flat.

Looking in the mirror one morning, I realized that a visit to a barber was past due. The situation was not urgent, but there were a few hairs on the top that needed trimming.

Finding Pammi in the hall at work that morning, I asked him how one went about getting a haircut in India. Pammi said to leave the matter to him. I went on with my work. Later that morning a note from Pammi was left on my desk.

"You must meet a man named Ravi in the hotel saloon at 5:30 p.m." There was no further explanation.

I left work a few minutes early in order to be on time for the appointment and proceeded directly to the hotel bar. It was empty. Ordering a beer, I asked the attendant if anyone had been inquiring for me. He was quite sure no one had. I handed him twenty rupees and asked if he would send the individual to my table when he arrived. A group of British expatriates crashed through the bar door to watch the televised rugby match. I nursed my beer and waited.

Six o'clock—"Would you like another round, sir?" the attendant asked.

Six-thirty—It seemed obvious I had been stood up.

Frustrated, and still wanting to do something productive with my time, I asked, "Is there a place in the hotel where I can have my hair cut?"

"Certainly, we have a *saloon* in the basement. Would you like me to call and arrange an appointment for you. There may be an opening now. Just take the stairway down to the left and ask for Ravi.

"I see, hmmm—*saloon*, hmmm…. This isn't a saloon?"

"No sir, this is the bar. The saloon is on the lower level."

"Hmmm—I see. Er—I might have called that a salon, but usually I go to a barber shop for a haircut."

"Oh, sir. Is it? I will make the arrangements. You just go down to the *saloon.*"

I went to see Ravi.

The episode began with barber Ravi using a rapid pulsing water nozzle, undoubtedly better than any fire extinguisher on the subcontinent, to fully soak the few lonely hairs that still had residence on the top of my head. Next, the barber spent about 40 minutes trimming and retrimming those hairs. This was followed by another treatment from the fire extinguisher, and what is best described as the individual towel drying of each hair. Towel drying evolved into a full scalp massage which continued down the shoulders. Not knowing what to expect next, I was planning my exit when Ravi made two quick slaps on the back of my head and placed hot towels over my face. The hairs, though already dry, were stirred up with an industrial-strength electric blow dryer. Finally, each hair was expertly combed across the top of my head. Never was so much done for so few!

"Thank you, Ravi." I pulled a rupee note from my wallet and paid the bill, happily including an attractive tip for this *"artist of the shears."*

6

2

Heaven and Hell

" 'I reckon some folks have to get used to worse places,' Bernard remarked toward the close of his first week at Shangri-La, and it was doubtless one of the many lessons to be drawn."

—James Hilton
from *Lost Horizons*

India is a land of contrasts. It is one spot on the earth where the past meets the future in its extremes, and where this mixture touches every facet of life. Coming to India as an outsider made the contrast more apparent, perhaps, than it would be to an individual spending a lifetime in the Indian culture.

One visitor put it simply, "India is like heaven and it is like hell."

Some of the contrasts we encountered may have been recognized in an effort to connect with our own lifestyle as we were learning to exist in India.

In 1998 a state-of-the-art cellular phone could be purchased and made functional in India in one day. At the other end of the spectrum, it could take more than two years for an Indian to advance through the waiting list for a traditional telephone connection and having made it to the front of the queue, it was likely to take another six weeks of persistent follow-up to wade through the bureaucratic red tape required to get the beast installed and operational.

During our stay, Bangalore was known as the leading center for technology in India. It was also the home of ISRO, the Indian Satellite Research Organization. For a country of its size and setting, India maintained an impressive space program. The institute was a complex of buildings protected by a tall security fence that enclosed the compound. Tropical trees and flowering vegetation surrounded the property, creating a serene setting. Armed guards protected the gate as scientists, businessmen, and politicians passed through on motor scooters, in cars, and on foot. This center was a technology jewel in India's crown. It was not uncommon to see supplies being delivered to the institute on a cart with wooden wheels, pulled by a bull with painted horns and a decorative bell dangling from the end of each horn. I often imagined that in the effort to produce a satellite, the nuts and bolts made at least one leg of their journey by ox cart.

My responsibilities on this expatriate assignment were to transfer technology and to help put an infrastructure in place that would allow our Indian subsidiary to do a greater volume of work than it had been doing, with greater complexity than it had been capable of, and with world-class standards. Since this involved an expansion of the workforce, a new network of computer workstations equipped with the latest in computer graphics capabilities was required. The engineering department would consume the entire second and third floors of an office building on RV Road in Basavanagudi, a district in Bangalore.

Desks and office partitions were required for the computers. One might expect that these could be purchased as routinely manufactured office furniture. Furnishings like this, however, were not commercially available in Bangalore at the time. They could only be custom built. A team of carpenters was dispatched from Calcutta. They lived on the roof of our office building for three months and built desks. Although they were hard at work, we did not see much of these fellows. They were like phantoms during office hours. Occasionally the leader and his young apprentice would appear in the hallway to take a measurement of sorts. The man would turn to face me, place his hands together, and nod in a traditional greeting. The carpenters cooked on the roof. They ate on the roof. They slept on the roof. They were in their own world which connected to ours by the need for a measurement now and then.

One morning, expecting to see a number of sawhorses, a supply of plywood, trim molding and other material, surrounded by a flurry of activity involving tape measures, electric saws, hand drills, and sanders, I walked up the last set of stairs in the building and opened the door to the roof. A number of barefoot carpenters were at work making trim molding and other boards. They were making the boards to make the desks! The tools they used required no electricity; a cross-cut saw, a rip saw, several other saws that were unfamiliar and more primitive, several chisels and gouges, a handmade plane, a draw knife, and a hand drill. In a setting where power availability was unpredictable, they could continue to work with no dependency on electricity.

The hand drill fascinated me. The carpenters might have been expected to be one generation of drilling technology behind the hand-held variable speed electric drill. If so, they would be using a manual drill with a geared hand crank, and a chuck with jaws that could accept a twist drill bit. In fact, a machine of that style would have been considered quite a step up for the carpenters. Their drill used a flat-pointed bit. The machine itself was a round, wooden spindle with a knob on the top and the flat bit driven into the spindle bottom. A separate wooden bow incorporated a rope that wrapped around the spindle. By moving the bow back and forth, the spindle turned clockwise and counterclockwise, and the flat bit produced a hole in the board beneath.

Cathy knew I was fascinated by this drill. She asked our driver to stop by the market to pick one up for me.

The driver returned from the market, "Madam, you cannot buy a drill. A drill is something that must be made."

"Who makes the drill?"

"The carpenter who uses the drill, madam."

"Let's have the carpenter make one for Dan."

"Yes madam. I will get it done."

Several weeks later, Cathy presented me with a brand new, nineteenth-century drill. Not long after that, partitions and desks began to mysteriously appear on the engineering floor. It was amazing. The desks had surfaces of cream-colored Formica. They were trimmed in expertly-polished rosewood. The drawers fit precisely in their openings and were equipped with locks identical to those on my desk in Michigan. The partitions had rosewood frames, and fabric interiors intended as surfaces for pinning up reference blueprints needed by the computer operators. These were first-class desks and partitions. The resulting office cubicles were as nice as those produced anywhere.

I shifted the chair back from my new desk, stared at the ceiling, and considered the contrast. A state-of-the-art computer network was being installed. The computers were resting on desks built by carpenters who lived on the roof for three months, who made the boards to make the desks, and who drilled with a mechanism that looked like it was used by Boy Scouts to start fires. A lizard darted across the ceiling to the corner of the room. I rolled up a print to help herd the creature out of the building.

Unpredictable electricity was one factor contributing to the survival of manual mechanization in India. In Bangalore, energy shortages frequently resulted in planned power outages that rotated around the city in four-hour blocks of time. Invariably, each day also included six or more additional hours of unplanned power outages. Each home and business had its own way of surviving without power. Some had generators. Most did not.

Bangalore was a place where it was still easier to buy a hand-tailored suit than to get one off the shelf. You could step off the broken sidewalk on Commercial Street and into a modern store with single-pane windows covering the entire exterior wall, select from the finest wool or silk, and be measured by a neatly dressed man with impeccable manners and a jovial personality. Three days after selecting a style and fabric, you would return for the final fitting of the garment. The store owner would ask whether you would like tea, or a glass of Thums Up, the traditional Indian cola. While you enjoyed this required business hospitality, the owner would send his helper to the street to fetch the tailor, who could make note of any final corrections that were necessary. A slight man in a dhoti was likely to come through the back of the shop and acknowledge you with a respectful bow, mark the fabric with chalk in several spots, exchange a brief sentence or two with the owner in Kannada, and scurry back to his sewing machine on one of the narrow alleys nearby. His sewing machine was likely to be powered by foot. The machine may have been new, but it was identical in every respect to what Singer first produced in 1918. Work would not stop for the tailor when power went out.

The Windsor Manor catered heavily to foreign travelers and had a good backup system for power outages. When searching for more permanent accommodations, it did not take long for us to realize we would be better off in an apartment than in a house because of the backup power infrastructure existing in the luxury apartment complexes in Bangalore. We settled in a delightful complex called Belvedere Court, in Bangalore's Fraser Town district, on a street called Spencer Road. This sounded quite ordinary compared to the typical Indian names that identify most of the city— such as Rajajinagar, Visveswarapuram, Jayamahal, and Basavanagudi. It made for easy letter addressing from the USA but didn't have quite the exotic ring to it that we had imagined. The complex had security guards at the entrance, spacious living areas, a courtyard with a finely manicured tropical garden, and a huge backup generator.

During our first week in the flat, we smelled a burning aroma coming from our building. We were somewhat concerned that the building was on fire because of stories we had read in the press. We had little confidence in the safety of wiring in any building in India. The smell was of such concern that I began to hunt for its source. Following my nose, I made my way down to the car-park area in the basement of the building. A thin cloud of smoke filled the air. I walked toward the power distribution enclosure, expecting to discover flames jumping from one of the panels. Much to my surprise, there was a small man in a corner bending over an old wooden table ironing clothes. In fact, some of the shirts belonged to me! This man was an expert at ironing. He would iron shirts, pants, place mats, tablecloths, underwear, socks, and anything else that he was given. The curious thing was that he used an iron heated with burning coals. Not only was it surprising to find this ancient device being used today, it was shocking to find it in one of Bangalore's most modern apartment facilities. Later that day I thought of buying the man an electric iron. Returning to his area to look around, there wasn't an electrical outlet to be found. It was easy to realize that the small man was better off with the coal iron because of the power predicament. A light green lizard scurried out of sight behind the power distribution panel near the wooden ironing table.

The traditional car used in India was the Hindustan Ambassador. Like the sewing machine, the Ambassador was still produced using the technology of 1930. The Ambassador was a simple vehicle that had impressed global automobile manufacturers by its ability to continue running in the face of Indian driving and road conditions. Drivers who had spent their lives in India were not as mystified as the Japanese, Korean, and American car producers. The Ambassador's thick sheet metal was tank-like armor useful in encountering the bumps and scrapes of chaotic Indian city traffic. A bullet proof version of the Ambassador was also produced. The ground clearance was equivalent to an All-Terrain Vehicle, allowing the Ambassador to make it through potholes, ditches, and rivers unharmed. Because it had been produced for more than fifty years, the Ambassador could be repaired in any rural village with resources that could be scraped together locally.

When our car—a new Tata Estate—arrived, it was the only model of car available in India at the time with factory mounted air conditioning and enough space to fit three adults and four children in a somewhat organized fashion. We hired a full-time driver, Selvan, to shuffle the vehicle through the traffic between the office, school, shops, and generally around southern India. This car and driver were our means of seeing rural India, and it allowed us to witness what were probably the two most striking demonstrations of contrast during our stay.

The first involved the improvement of the rural highways. Because vehicles were shifting from the Ambassador, which could drive across a dirt path without much trouble, to more modern Suzukis, Daewoos, and Fords, and because personal automobile transportation was becoming more common, road surface improvement and repair were required. On many occasions in our travels, we came across road improvement teams. A team consisted of a small group of about eight people living in a tent at the roadside. They built or repaired several meters of road each day. The process began with a pile of football-size granite blocks dropped near the area being worked. Two men, whose job it was to break the blocks into gravel-size stone, were hard at work swinging heavy wooden handled sledgehammers. Women with baskets carried the gravel on their heads to a spot in the road where it was spread in a heavy blanket for the road base. Nearby, an oil drum that had been cut in half lengthwise and welded to an angle iron stand was filled with tar. A wood fire burned under the half barrel to heat and soften the black mixture. One man dipped a cuplike ladle into the pot and spread tar on the gravel cup by cup. At the right time, a small diesel-powered rolling vehicle flattened the surface to make it drivable. The result, though not the same quality we were used to on new roads in America, was an improvement of extraordinary proportion. A Mercedes Benz in rural India travels on a surface where gravel was made by hand, and tar was applied by teacup.

The second demonstration of contrast was a project taking place on a vast scale across the country, through rural areas and cities alike. Along each main road a deep trench was being dug using shovels and picks. With small teams of about a dozen workers living in tents on the roadside as they went, and using only simple hand tools, a large fiber-optic communication cable, intended to provide the skeleton for India's domestic phone system, was being imbedded in the ground. Similar to the carpenters at my office, the men and women digging the trench—living in camplike conditions and using resources that would not be considered for a project of much smaller scale in Europe or America—were making it possible for India to introduce the latest technology and leap forward in one gigantic step.

3

Ancient Times

"In no country in the world has geographical position, relative to surrounding continents and seas, shaped the history and the destinies of the people more surely than in India."

—Sir T. H. Holdich

When the formation of the earth as we know it began, with land masses separating into continents, plates below the earth's surface shifted to force layer after layer of strata toward the heavens, and icy glaciers found their homes near jagged Himalayan peaks. A small stream began as a trickle from melting glacier ice on a mountain in Tibet. The stream meandered down the mountainside and joined a larger stream known as the Indus. As it flowed northwest first, through what is now India's Jammu and Kashmir frontier, the Indus picked up water from the mountain sides of K2 and Rakaposhi before making a bend to the left around another monster peak, Nanga Parbat, and heading as a fully mature river on a southern trajectory through what is now Pakistan, eventually emptying into the Arabian Sea.

A second river, the Saraswati, now extinct, followed a path parallel to but west of the Indus. Together they created the Indus Valley. Evidence of Stone Age human life in this region can be traced back nearly 700,000 years, when small bands of hunters inhabited isolated areas on the Indian subcontinent. As one of these clans of people, hunting in the northern Indus Valley, grew, and individuals became increasingly dependent upon each other, their culture developed into a civilization, one of the earliest on earth.

By 7000 BCE, a small agricultural settlement, Mehrgarh, had evolved in the region, with domesticated animals and planted crops easing the effort of survival. By 2600 BCE, the Indus Valley was the home of several urban population centers and a civilization that relied on urban technology, specialized craftsmanship, and trade that extended west as far as Mesopotamia. Excavations have unearthed two major cities of the period, Mohenjodaro and Harappa, commerce hubs with influence well beyond the subcontinent. In fact, detailed cuneiform texts from Mesopotamia provide evidence that raw materials and objects from the Indus Valley were carried by ships to Mesopotamia as early as 2350 BCE.

The communities inhabiting the Indus Valley from about 2600 BCE until about 1800 BCE are now known as the Harappan civilization. While some theories have been offered about Harappan written texts, modern scholars have been unable to agree fully with each other on a deciphered translation of the pictogram script used by this Bronze Age civilization. The culture's influence spread throughout the western edge of the Indian subcontinent, with more than 1,000 towns and cities dating back to about 2000 BCE found as far south as the Deccan Plateau, and as far east as Delhi. The brick construction of dwellings and storage facilities in these settlements included deliberate architectural features. The locations of the building structures appear to have been part of overall city planning. At Harappa, the city includes a walled fortress, which may indicate the presence of military planning. Within the urban centers of

Harappa and Mohenjodaro, archaeologists have found that the Harappans had developed ventilation ducts inside their buildings, cylindrical wells, wastewater drainage, flour grinding, grain storage, and other technologies for improving the quality of life.

After nearly 800 years of continuous flourishing life and culture, the massive urban centers of Harrapa and Mohenjodero were deserted in a relatively short period of time. The reason for the sudden decline is somewhat of a mystery. One plausible explanation suggests that several factors combined to cause the collapse. First, for many decades the cities themselves flourished, but eventually they became overpopulated. The overpopulation resulted in slum-like conditions on the outskirts of the cities at around 1800 BCE. Archaeologists have noted a decrease in the standard of living at this stage of the cities' existence. Second, a significant shift in the terrain occurred in about the same time period. The Saraswati River, which supported several urban centers, abruptly dried up, perhaps due to an earthquake. Water from the Himalayas shifted to the Indus, thereby starving cities on the Saraswati and flooding cities on the Indus. As population rapidly migrated from the cities that were no longer practical to inhabit, the problem of overpopulation was amplified in cities that could be used. Eventually food resources were inadequate to sustain the large number of inhabitants.

The weakened social structure also resulted in an inadequate defense infrastructure, exposing the Harappan populations to invasion from tribes crossing through the Himalayan passes. Linguistic evidence suggests that the people of the Harappan civilization were eventually displaced by nomadic, warring Indo-Aryans migrating from the steppes of Eurasia, between southern Russia and Turkey.

From a glacier on the side of Annapurna, a mountain in what is now Nepal, another stream trickled down into a valley to form a small mountain river, the Gandok. Collecting water from other sources on its journey between giant peaks in Nepal, the river found a way into the northern plateau of the Indian subcontinent and poured itself into a larger river, the Ganga. Flowing due east, the Ganga collected water from similar streams flowing down from Everest, Kanchenjunga, and other lofty peaks, becoming a mighty stream, heading toward the Bay of Bengal.

The River Ganga, or Ganges River as it is commonly called outside of India, became the life source for a new group of civilized people that appeared around 1800 BCE, a group influenced by migration from the Indus Valley, yet unique in their impact on today's world. As the Indo-Aryan warlike nomads merged with the displaced Harrapan settlers migrating to the plains of the Ganga, a new culture emerged, giving rise to the Vedic period in Indian history, 1800–600 BCE. The Vedic culture laid the foundation for Hinduism, one of the predominant religions in today's world. Several historical, philosophical, and practical works were passed down in oral tradition and later written in Sanskrit. These literary accomplishments are certainly some of the most influential achievements of the Vedic age.

It is thought that the integration of the Indo-Aryan warlike culture with the Harappan trade and agricultural society resulted in social stratification, leading to regional kingdoms with powerful individual rulers, as well as the class segregation of India's caste system. The language adopted during this period by the people in the Indus and Ganga regions was an Indo-Aryan language, a precursor to Sanskrit which linguists have also linked to Dravidian, a language believed to have been derived from the tongue of the Harrapans.

During the Vedic period several technologies and disciplines were introduced to or developed by the people of the subcontinent. For instance, the domesticated horse was brought to the Indus region by Indo-Aryans from southern Russia. It is thought that the chariot was also introduced to the subcontinent with the migration of Aryans from the steppes of central Eurasia during the second millennium BCE. The earliest-known form of martial art, Kalirippayat, originated in present-day Kerala, India, during the Vedic period. It was eventually introduced to China by a traveling monk in about 600 BCE, where it is thought to have evolved into kung fu. An improved form of pottery, Painted Grey Ware, first appeared in India during the Vedic period. Society during this time demonstrated significant advancement in agricultural methods, animal breeding, weaponry, and military techniques.

One day, perhaps between 480 and 400 BCE, a prince was born in the Northern India kingdom of Sakka. When he was an infant, the local soothsayers predicted that he would leave his family to become a wandering ascetic and religious teacher. When this king-to-be was twenty-nine years old, he took a chariot ride from the palace through a local park. On the outing, Siddhartha Gautama came across a frail man suffering from old age. Gautama was taken aback by what he saw. The following day, when Gautama visited the same park, he encountered a sick man. For the first time Gautama confronted the reality of life, from which his father, the king, had shielded him. On the third day Gautama saw a corpse. When, on the fourth day, Gautama, perplexed by the natural suffering of the human condition, encountered a robed, head-shaven man who seemed content with the simplicity of his being, Gautama left his luxurious surroundings, his wife and young son to adopt a lifestyle of wandering and meditation. It was on this journey that Gautama sat for 49 days under a pipal (bodhi) tree in northern India until he reached enlightenment. Buddhism was born. Buddhism is one of the foremost achievements of India's 600–100 BCE time period, the Pre-Mauryan and Mauryan age.

During this period, in 326 BCE, an invading army of 120,000 soldiers and 15,000 horses crossed what are now the Hindu Kush mountains of Afghanistan and marched into the Indian subcontinent, conquering one kingdom after another. They battled fiercely against Indian armies, who fought on elephant. The invaders slaughtered thousands but, in many cases, returned the kingdom to the submissive ruler, thereby establishing an alliance in the region. In one surprise attack the leader of the invaders was the first to jump from a wall into his enemy's fort. An arrow sailed through the air and pierced the young hero's breastplate and penetrated his ribs. He continued to fight until fainting from lack of blood. The battle continued, with Alexander the Great unconscious and protected by his bodyguards, until the fort was conquered. Alexander recovered and in time returned to Macedonia with only a quarter of the force he had brought into India. During his Indian campaign, Alexander was heartbroken when Bucephalus, the horse he had ridden into every battle of his conquest, was wounded and died. Having established numerous alliances on the subcontinent, and having met with India's chieftains and philosophers, Alexander left behind his reputation, his ideas, and ambassadors to promote trade. He wove a Greek influence into the fabric of India's history.

An ancient city, Pataliputra, located at the confluence of the Ganga and Ganduk rivers, whose ruins have been partially excavated from the silt on which present day Patna is built, was the capital of the first empire unifying all of northern India. Chandragupta Maurya founded a dynasty in 325 BCE which lasted until 185 BCE and not only consolidated the small kingdoms of the region, but also promoted trade from as far west as Egypt, and east throughout southeast Asia. Chandragupta Maurya's grandson and king of the empire, Ashoka, developed and expanded the empire until it reached its apex, with borders across the entire northern region and extending south to Mysore. Archaeologists have found pillars throughout Ashoka's empire inscribed with a code of law and morality that was disseminated across the domain.

During his rule, Ashoka became a Buddhist. While tolerant of all religions throughout the empire, he personally encouraged Buddhism and sent missionaries throughout the subcontinent and into Asia. Ashoka's son and daughter were sent as Buddhist missionaries to Ceylon (today, Sri Lanka). It was Ashoka who commissioned sculptors to erect a pillar at Sarnath featuring four lions sitting back-to-back on the pillar's capital, a symbol that even today represents the Republic of India. During his reign, trade flourished from the Mediterranean to Asia, and a cultural integration of technologies, architecture, and customs is believed to have existed. Ashoka is known to have set up hospitals, veterinary clinics and other infrastructure improvements within the empire.

The glory of the Mauryan period, however, was short lived. Less than five decades after the death of Ashoka, the last heir of the Mauryan dynasty was assassinated, and the empire that had established the unification of the subcontinent was again divided into a group of smaller kingdoms.

Invading armies of Bactrians, Scythians, Parthians, and Kushanas conquered and reconquered portions of northern India. Meanwhile, in the south, a new dynasty, the Satavahanas, emerged and unified southern India from the Deccan Plateau to the southern tip of the peninsula. During the Satavahana period, 100 BCE–300 CE, a distinctive construction of Buddhist and Jain cave monasteries began. In this era, the first of India's cave temples, many hand-carved in shear bedrock, were constructed on ancient trade routes. The structures served as active monasteries and rest spots for wealthy travelers. Construction was funded by patronage from the travelers, who, in return for their contribution, knew they would have a place to stop on their next journey. Construction of an early site, Ajanta, began near the end of the Satavahana period. The Ajanta cave surfaces have been painted with full murals depicting elements of Buddhism. Construction of impressive cave temples continued well into the ninth century CE. Lost for hundreds of years, many of the caves, when rediscovered in the dense Indian jungle, were amazingly intact.

During the Satavahana period, archaeological and literary evidence indicates that a strong trading relationship existed between the Roman Empire and India. During the first century CE, after more than 100 years of successive invasions from the north by a variety of intruders, the Kushanas, a group from central Asia, conquered all of northern India and established an empire, bringing a Chinese influence to the region. When the empire reached its peak, King Kanishka controlled all the major trade routes of the Silk Road, which linked China with the Roman Empire. This was a time of stability in Northern India, and the prosperity and tranquility of the time inspired a notable surge in

23

craftsmanship and aesthetic benevolence. Two centers of sculpture developed during this time, one at Gandhara and one at Mathura, each producing architectural products of superb craftsmanship, and showing evidence of Roman, Chinese, and Indian influence.

By the middle of the third century CE, the Kushana empire was overthrown by invaders from Persia. Several decades later, a local chieftain living on the border that now separates the states of Bihar and Bengal arranged for the marriage of his son, Chandragupta I, to a princess from a territory near the southern border of present-day Nepal. Chandragupta I is known to be one of India's greatest rulers. His conquest again united all of northern India and was the beginning of India's brief Golden Age. The Gupta Empire, 300–500 CE, brought to India a period of prosperity, artistic expression and intellectual inspiration. Under the reign of Chandragupta I's son, Samudragupta, the empire in the north expanded south into the Deccan Plateau.

At the same time a parallel empire, the Vakataka Empire, had been formed to unite southern India. The two kingdoms coexisted peacefully, together controlling the entire subcontinent. Religious and intellectual ideas and trade flowed freely between the two empires, and there was an integration of northern and southern nobility through marriage.

In 476 CE, perhaps in a small town in Kerala, one of India's southern states, a boy was born. Although little is known about the early life of Aryabhata, when he reached the age of 23, he was living close to Pataliputra, writing some of history's most brilliant astronomical and mathematical works. Aryabhata is credited for having developed an approximation of pi, accurate to the 8th decimal point. He defined the length of a year as 365 days, 6 hours, 12 minutes and 30 seconds, which is an overestimation by 3 minutes and 20.5 seconds. Aryabhata's contributions to pure mathematics include a table of trigonometric sines, and mathematical rules addressing arithmetic, algebra, and plane and spherical trigonometry. Aryabhata had also deduced that the earth was a sphere rotating on an axis and revolving around the sun. He believed that the moon and planets were visible because of reflected light, and that the movement of the stars in the sky as seen from earth was in fact due to the rotation of the earth on its axis. Aryabhata knew that planetary orbits followed elliptical paths around the sun.

During the Gupta period, Arabic numerals and decimal notation were developed by Indian mathematicians. While religious tolerance existed during this Golden Age of the Guptas, Buddhism declined and was replaced almost entirely by Hinduism. Freestanding Hindu temples that can still be seen today were constructed in the north. At the same time, Hindu and Jain cave temples continued to be developed in the south at places like Elephanta, Ajanta, and Ellora.

In the end, leadership of both the Gupta empire and the Vakataka empire weakened, and the entire subcontinent fragmented into smaller kingdoms, exposing it once again to the danger of invaders from the north. Feudalism resulting from the collapse of the Gupta and Vakataka empires lasted for hundreds of years, until the Vijayanagar empire emerged in central India during the 14th century CE as a global hub for commerce and culture.

4

Expecting the Unexpected

"The world is full of obvious things which nobody by any chance ever observes."

—Sir Arthur Conan Doyle
from *The Hound of the Baskervilles*

Our stay in the Windsor Manor lasted nearly one month. In spite of the elegance the place offered, we were beginning to feel cabin fever after a couple of weeks. Because of the manicured atmosphere in the hotel, nothing less than sharp casual attire was appropriate. The children didn't have a place where they could cut loose. As best we could, we made plans for weekend outings.

On our last Sunday at the Windsor Manor, we got up in the morning and decided to take a drive into the countryside. This also turned out to be the morning that the prime minister of India, the head of the state of Karnataka, the mayor of Bangalore, and a high ranking official from the United Nations were all meeting at the hotel. Several military generals strolled formally across the lobby. The children, who had taken a separate elevator down from the room, made it to the main floor just as the big brass walked into the same area. My son, Kirk, only five years old, dashed out of the elevator and ran directly into a high-ranking general who was standing with his back to the elevator. It was like a squirrel released in a gourmet kitchen. Kirk darted from one person to the next as they reached down to pat him on the head. He looked like a steel marble in a pin-ball machine, making a beeline from object to object, trying to find us in the commotion. We finally caught Kirk and were quickly escorted out the back of the hotel where security officials had redirected our car and driver.

This political entourage caused a considerable fuss in Bangalore since the main roads from the airport had to be cleared to allow the prime minister's caravan of vehicles to make it safely to the hotel. It meant mobilizing hundreds of traffic directors and military personnel. The event resulted in an unusual tranquility on the main artery between the airport and the Windsor Manor. It also resulted in mass chaos in every other sector of the city.

Bangalore was proud of its main golf course. It was situated opposite the Windsor Manor and was not far from the city's horse racetrack. This was one of only two golf courses in our part of India. The city golf course was unique. It occupied a fairly small patch of land. Several of the fairways teed off north to south. Others half teed off east to west. Some of the fairways used the same space as they crisscrossed each other. Tee times were staggered to mitigate some of the safety issues.

Lawn maintenance on the fairway of the golf course was interesting. The mower was simply a reel-type device, with perhaps one meter of cutting width. Two ropes were attached to the front with one person pulling each rope over his shoulder. A third person steered the device from the rear. It was incredible that the entire fairway could be cut using this method. The grounds crew must have been happy that the fairways crisscrossed each other, sharing the same patch of grass. The small mounds that surrounded the greens and sand traps were cut by a group of ladies in saris with scythes and hand clippers.

From the beginning we had a hard time finding our way around Bangalore. Some of this was to be expected and would have happened in any new location. It was difficult to give directions and to follow directions that we were given. At first this seemed to be a result of the fact that there were so few street signs positioned around the city. We eventually realized that even if there were street signs, it would have been confusing since the street names changed in the city nearly every kilometer.

Traffic was wonderful. After 10:00 a.m. Bangalore became a giant free-for-all, with traffic moving in both directions on both sides of the street. Horns were used for communication rather than emergencies, and the rare traffic signals were only marginally obeyed. What sounded like it had all the makings of a near-death situation was actually not much more lethal than a loud conversation. Everything seemed to work because it all happened at such a slow speed, and because all drivers had a tolerance for the situation. It was like life-size chess pieces creeping from one position to the next on a giant game board. Often after driving for half an hour in the city, our vehicle moved less than five kilometers.

Since horn communication in Bangalore was such an integral part of driving, it came as a surprise to find an article in the local newspaper, the Deccan Herald, stating that the city council was seriously concerned about the increase of noise pollution in Bangalore. The main concern focused on noise pollution from horns continuously being sounded by trucks, buses, cars, and auto-rickshaws. The council was so concerned about the noise pollution that it funded a special squad to identify loud horns and hand out fines or impound vehicles. The council passed a resolution that anyone who had a horn exceeding 130 decibels would be fined. Five college students and one part-time police officer made up the squad assigned to the task. One instrument to properly measure sound levels was made available to the group. This team of superheroes was commissioned with the responsibility to enforce the new resolution citywide, covering a population of five million, very few of whom would make an honest effort to stop for a traffic signal.

Our slow driving speeds provided excellent opportunities to see life in the city. One morning we drove past a park where there was a game of cricket in process. As the game was being played, a water buffalo walked peacefully around the infield, munching on clumps of grass, and any other food that may have been in the area. The play carried on as if the buffalo was part of the field.

On another occasion, a man was walking six dogs: all on leashes. They walked six abreast in an even line ahead of the man. One of the dogs appeared to be limping a bit. As I got closer it was apparent that the animal in the middle was not a dog at all. It was a monkey, and it was skipping along on two legs and one arm, as monkeys do, with a chain around its waist rather than a neck collar. The menagerie looked strange as it passed. It was unusual to see a monkey with a leash around its waist in with a pack of dogs. After a short time, a sharp yipe sounded. The monkey was yanking at one of the dogs' tails. This quickly evolved into a massive entanglement with growls, screeches, and squeals. Before things were finally under control, there was a great wrestling match with monkey, dog, and man.

Men and women on the city streets were often seen carrying large bags of goods on their heads, sometimes balancing two or three bags without using their hands. One morning while waiting for traffic to clear at an intersection, a cow ate the entire paper surface off a billboard. The city had many loose cows that would use any open patch of green as pasture. There was even a cow patrol in the city that had the job to pick up stray cattle and remove them from *cow-free* zones. Two days later, arriving at the same intersection, the same cow and its cousin had claimed the crossroads area. One cow wandered around peacefully, looking hungrily at the billboards. The other was quite frisky. Whenever a person stepped into the street, the frisky cow curled its neck, pointed its horns forward, and made a charge at the pedestrian. In general, the cow was attacking people from behind, and most of the people weren't aware that the cow was after them until it was almost too late. This made for several good sprints, long jumps, and other acrobatic moves to make it safely to the sidewalk. There were three crosswalks in this intersection, and the cow charged from one to the next in bull-fighting mode to keep the pedestrians out of its newly claimed territory. People on the sidelines finally figured out what the cow's intentions were and surrendered the intersection to its new land baron.

There was also the other extreme from time to time. One day we pulled up to an intersection and waited for instructions from a white-gloved police officer who was about to direct our batch of vehicles to proceed. One of the slowest-moving cows in Bangalore began to make its way across the intersection. When the officer finally motioned for us to advance, the cow had managed to be positioned directly in front of our vehicle. It was millimeters from the grill. The cow would not budge. Cars behind were honking. We could not back up. We tooted our horn, trying to communicate with the bovine and to encourage it to get out of the way. As I opened the car door, intending to drag the beast to the median, the cow

30

moved—perhaps one centimeter…and then another centimeter. It looked around—one more centimeter.

As luck would have it, the big black cow was almost clear of our front end when the officer stopped our lane to let the other direction of traffic proceed. We had plenty of frustrated drivers behind us, many of whom didn't give a whit about the instructions of the traffic officer. We sat and waited for the next round. After a while the officer waved us on again, just as the cow, which had managed to creep to about a meter clear of our car, turned its head with intentions of returning to block our vehicle again. We made a quick dash beyond the cow and left the bovine to be someone else's problem. This was life in Bangalore.

Someone was always pushing the safety envelope a bit further. A few days later while we were traveling through this free-for-all, a small motor scooter carrying four people moved along next to our vehicle. The man driving the scooter had a child of about eight years old sitting on his lap. A woman in a sari was sitting side-saddle on the back carrying a four-year-old. There were no helmets, of course. Nearly a month later we saw a motorcycle carrying five people. Three months later we saw a motorcycle carrying three men and two live goats.

After a few weeks in India, I decided to bring the whole family to my office in Basavanagudi. As a special treat, and as a way to break free of our Windsor Manor routine, the plan included eating an American buffet breakfast at another of Bangalore's prominent hotels. Evidently our youngest son, Kirk, did not fully understand the agenda. When we pulled up to the magnificent entry of the Oberoi Hotel, complete with doormen in uniforms sporting large, curled mustaches, marble stairs, six-meter ceilings, sprawling gardens, and floor-to-ceiling windows, his eyes widened like saucers and he enthusiastically exclaimed, "Dad's office!" I wonder what he would have thought if we had stopped at the Taj Mahal on the way to the office.

Nearly eight weeks after arrival I knew it was time for me to take my chances on the streets of Bangalore behind the wheel of our Tata Estate. Selvan suggested Sunday, when traffic was the most tame. He sat in the front seat as copilot and coach. When Selvan arrived at about 8:00 a.m., we headed down the road for a leisurely drive around the tank, a small lake that also served as a reservoir for Bangalore.

As with many regions of British colonization, the primary side of the road for driving in India was the left. Most drivers from America and mainland Europe questioned their basic instinct at every intersection while driving on the left. The scary part about intersections in India, however, was that they were governed only by nature's law of size. Charles Darwin could have developed his theories of survival and evolution on the basis of vehicles in Bangalore alone. It was an unwritten rule that vehicles proceeded through unmarked intersections according to size. It made no difference how fast each vehicle was moving, the smallest had to wait. The largest was expected to nudge its way through. This rule applied to the few intersections with traffic signals also, depending on the disposition of the driver at the front of the line. At times traffic signals appeared to be nothing more than ornaments. Still, the fundamental rule always worked. Smaller vehicles let the bigger vehicles go by. Bigger vehicles did not confuse smaller vehicles by stopping. The strong survived. Those who broke the natural rule perished!

On the open road, the game of leapfrog and chicken were common; here, also, people followed the unwritten pecking order among vehicles. Trucks and buses did as they pleased, next came cars, then auto-rickshaws, bicycles, and finally humans. Everyone gave way to horses, cows, buffalo, donkeys, dogs and the occasional monkey, all of which roamed the streets, eating the grass in the median and sleeping in parking spaces.

After finishing the loop around the tank, I told Selvan that I intended to practice a drive to the office and back. A look of terror flashed across his face. We had to go through some of the busiest sections of the city and he was not prepared to navigate these as a passenger.

Selvan coached me along the way.

"Left here…Right here…This is a one-way road, sir! Stop now! Don't stop!"

We snaked through roundabouts, up small alleys, and, with a final U-turn, ended up in front of the office in Basavanagudi. Selvan was hoping he could drive back to the flat. We filled the car with diesel, and much to Selvan's dismay, I inched my way through Bangalore one more time, retracing our path and finally arriving at our flat with white knuckles and a passenger who very seriously wanted to have the rest of the day off from work.

Our flat was equipped with five air conditioners. Central air conditioning was not available in India at the time. The catch to air conditioners in India was that most dwellings did not have enough power to operate them. Many places were serviced with only 2 KW of power. By luck, our apartment had 9 KW. Even so, when the power went out, which it did on a planned basis for four hours each day, and the apartment complex's generator came on, only lights and some electronic equipment could be operated. Each flat had circuits of two types: one that was generator-powered during an outage, and one that was not. Refrigerators, water heaters, and air conditioners required too much power to be operated by the generator.

Many household items in India were designed to accommodate power outages. For instance, the refrigerator in the flat had four separate doors, so that when the power went out, there was no need to open the whole refrigerator and let any more cold air out than was necessary. Water heaters were also different from the American variety. People in Bangalore called them geezers. Each was set up to service only one water tap. We had four geezers in our apartment: one in each bathroom, and one in the kitchen. Each of the geezers had to be turned on manually about half an hour before hot water was needed. The geezers hung on the wall near the ceiling, each holding about 20 liters of water, which turned out to be more than enough to take a shower or two. If we turned on too many geezers at once, the main power in the flat would cut out. If we operated two air conditioners and one geezer at the same time, power would cut out. If the refrigerator compressor happened to start when the wrong combination of appliances was running, power would cut out. We had to decide constantly when to run the air conditioners, the geezers, the television, or the computer. The process was entirely manual. The upside of this process was that it conserved energy, which was one thing India needed. It became a way of life for us, as it was with all people living in India who were fortunate enough to have electricity.

Limited electricity also made electric clothes dryers somewhat impractical. Most clothes were hang-dried. People with automatic clothes driers are accustomed to losing an occasional sock while doing laundry. In India, without automatic dryers, it was mystifying that socks still turned up missing. Losing a sock in an automatic dryer didn't make much sense. This made even less. The clothes were routinely hung to dry on the balcony connected to the boys' bedroom. One sock would disappear, a single cloth napkin would be gone, each time it was an item that would be of little use on its own. One day Kirk lay in bed staring out the window. A large monkey swung down from a tree limb close by, bounced nimbly off the railing, and hopped up on to the clothes drying rack. The monkey looked around and fiddled with the clothes pins. It wasn't long before the creature took a pair of pants from the rack, slipped its fuzzy legs in and pulled the pants up to its chest. The monkey screeched and chattered, jumping around proudly, dropped the trousers, and left the balcony, taking one red wooden clothes pin with him. The mystery was solved.

The household helpers who worked in our flat had lives that were also touched with issues of energy conservation, but they were from homes that may have been without electricity all together. They certainly had no running water of their own, no telephone, and no modern provisions for cooking fuel at home. One day after returning from a particularly hot weekend trip, we opened our refrigerator to find its complete contents spoiled. We followed the trail of what could have caused this situation and found the appliance unplugged from the wall. Cathy asked the maid how this had happened. The woman proudly announced that she had unplugged the refrigerator, and every other device in the flat in order to conserve electricity while we were gone. It was logical.

The woman coming to our flat to help every day was to assist with cooking and cleaning. Cleaning was the main job; cooking was an added benefit. On the surface, this may sound like a real help, but there were as many cooking failures as successes. The first domestic assistant was a woman named June. She liked to spice things up a bit. She understandably imagined that we would like food best if it was cooked the way she liked it.

One day Cathy asked June to prepare the roast with gravy, following the same procedure that Cathy had shown her only one week earlier. I arrived home from work that day to an aroma that made me homesick for Sunday dinner cooked by my mother. Roast beef, mashed potatoes, gravy! When assigned the task of carving the roast, the meat had been placed on the cutting board, and much to my surprise had pieces of cinnamon projecting from its surface like a porcupine. I looked in horror at the roast that had been converted into a pin cushion with cinnamon needles and thought it may have been some sort of voodoo ritual thing. Cinnamon with a roast? Oh no! Who had heard of this before?

When we sat down at the table June brought the gravy. It looked like vegetable soup.

"I thought sir was looking skinny and he would eat more vegetables if I put them in the gravy!" June proclaimed proudly.

Help!

Another one of June's jobs was to keep the house plants alive. About every other week though, the plants would look like they were near death from lack of water. June always said it was the wrong kind of soil.

Hmm—this was the soil that the plants had grown in from the time they were born. We suggested that June water them every second day.

June drenched the plants. She watered them so aggressively that the water ran across the floor. June emphatically pointed out, "Sir, see what happens when I water them so often!"

One day she must have noticed several of the leaves shriveling. Lack of water, too much water, who knows! She attacked the plants with scissors. Cutting most of the leaves in half, she removed any part of a plant that was brown. We waited cautiously to see if this would actually bring the plants around. They looked pitiful and within one month were finally resting in peace. It must have been the soil.

June was eventually replaced. This was fine with me since her cooking was becoming its own type of adventure. When we got to the point that it seemed wise to hire a food taster, we figured it was probably better to fire the cook than to build up the household staff. Actually, the problem was that June really liked to cook and didn't like to clean. We needed her to clean, but she had her own mind made up about how that was going to be done.

Our new assistant, Molly, came in for one month on a trial basis. Molly was a tiny woman no taller than 130 cm. No cooking this time—we had learned our lesson. Molly had been living with another expatriate family from Illinois. The family thought she was terrific at cleaning. The family needed live-in help, but Molly was getting married to an auto-rickshaw driver and needed to live with her new husband. Molly was a good replacement for June, since we were looking only for someone part-time. On the first day of work, Molly came to Cathy and asked how to use the elevator. We were taken aback. Molly was twenty years old and had never been in an elevator. The next day when I called home from the office, Molly was the only person in the flat. After picking up the receiver of the phone, she quickly hung up. Evidently, she was listening to the wrong end of the phone and when she could not hear a response, Molly responded by putting the phone back in its cradle.

Molly was an expert at house cleaning. She could also water plants.

Bangalore was known for its restaurants. It took us a while to find the ones that suited us. Frequently we would find small surprises that caught our attention and kept our interest in a particular restaurant. Rarely could we find a place that was good in every respect.

One evening Cathy noticed that the menu included French onion soup and decided excitedly to begin with a bowl. When the soup arrived, she began to spoon the broth from the top. The soup was good. Spooning deeper into the bowl she noticed an unfamiliar texture in her mouth, and discretely shifted the contents back into the bowl. Inspecting the soup further, Cathy set the spoon aside and shifted the bowl to the top of her place setting to wait for the main course.

The waiter arrived. "Madam, you didn't eat your soup."

"No, I'll just wait for the next course."

"But madam, is there something wrong with your soup?"

Looking palely at the bowl, Cathy shyly responded, "There seems to be a raw egg in my soup."

"Yes, madam. There is a raw egg in the soup."

"But I thought that this was French onion soup. I don't know that French onion soup is made with a raw egg."

"Oh yes, madam. That is because it is Chinese French onion soup."

We drank only purified bottled water in India, purchasing it three cases at a time. Even today, when we go to an Indian restaurant, the experience doesn't seem authentic without a bottle of Bisleri water sitting on the table. We did have a good purifier in the kitchen and one in each bathroom. These purifiers had physical filters as well as ultraviolet devices. Truthfully, they also played *Santa Claus is Coming to Town* when water was coming out. We used them for cleaning toothbrushes and similar things. Bottled water was the safest approach for drinking. Some of the diseases that could be caught in India from ordinary tap water were quite ugly to deal with. Even people who had lived in the area for their whole life and had built up an immunity to most of the local germs would from time to time end up with typhoid or hepatitis.

Beer, wine, and other alcoholic concoctions made in India were available in Bangalore. Some areas in India were dry. We eventually came to like several of the Indian beers well enough but still missed our old favorites. One day, when in Delhi for a short stretch, I opened the hotel's mini bar refrigerator in my room and found two large cans of Stroh's Beer. Stroh's beer! This was unbelievable. Milk from the Detroit River! What a treat. I looked at the blue can which was nearly the same as a Michigan can. The label said it was brewed in Rajasthan, a state near Delhi. A few months later I found a red can of Stroh's on the table of a restaurant in Bangalore. The proprietor said it was brought in from Rajasthan, but it was not for sale in Bangalore yet. Oh, a taste of home. What a delight!

Our Tata Estate was the only one in Bangalore with an "I Love Michigan State University" sticker in the rear window. The sticker allowed us to easily identify the vehicle. Most cars in the city were white, often making it hard to pick your own vehicle out of traffic. Ours had a roof rack so that we could all ride in the vehicle when we also needed to carry luggage. The thing looked a bit like a back-country vehicle.

A few days after adding the "I Love MSU sticker", Selvan must have been demonstrating his independence. In the morning there was a bright yellow sticker on the bumper that read "Get Rid of Jerks!" I was completely surprised that he had put this on the car without asking for approval in advance.

"What is this?" I asked.

Selvan proudly replied "A bumper sticker, sir!"

Hmm—what should be made of this? It required a day of thinking.

Finally, I asked Pammi, "Does jerk mean anything irreverent in India?"

Pammi chuckled and said, "No, Dan. Jerks are a kind of low-quality tire, and an American company is trying to introduce its new radials in India!"

Pammi thought there was no problem with leaving the sticker on the vehicle. So, our car then became the only vehicle in Bangalore with an alumni sticker in the window and "Get Rid of Jerks!" on the back bumper.

Not long after moving into our flat Cathy began taking Kannada lessons. Three or four weeks later she worked up the courage to practice her newly acquired skill on a family of potters that had taken up residence in a small tent on a street close by. These were typical street-side vendors, and their tent was made of rags and burlap. Needless to say, the prices for these pots were far from fixed. Blond hair and blue eyes could cause prices to escalate rapidly. Rupees must have flashed in the merchant's eyes, but when Cathy began to speak in the local language, the pot sellers were caught off guard. Things must have become a little mixed up as the bargaining progressed. Walking through the stock, Cathy asked about this pot, and then that pot, and pointed at still another. The price began at 4,000 rupees. The deal was finally struck with three pots purchased for 800 rupees. The merchant began loading the pots into the back of the Tata Estate. He put in the three pots Cathy had selected. He then brought another pot and placed it in the back, and then another, and another. Finally, all eight pots Cathy had inquired about were in the back of the vehicle.

"What is he doing?" Cathy asked Selvan. "I bought three pots!"

"No madam, you bought all the pots."

Having no idea exactly what she had done, Cathy thanked the merchant in Kannada and handed him eight 100-rupee notes. The man put his hands together and nodded in a traditional thanks as he accepted the cash. A small green lizard poked its head out of one of the pots in the car.

Occasionally Nick and I walked to a small park about six blocks from our flat in order to play basketball. This was a small park next to the railroad tracks. It was not in a good section of town. It didn't seem like anyone who lived in this area owned a basketball, and the two netless hoops in the little park were always available. The pavement surface was full of potholes and cracks.

When we arrived on one occasion, about 500 goats were grazing in the park. They filled the entire park, with the exception of the basketball court itself. The goats were in a queue for the stockyard several blocks down the road and were quite literally having their last supper. Nick and I pushed our way through the animals, shooed a few of the critters off the pavement, and began a game of one-on-one. Before long, four goat herders were paying more attention to our game than to the goats. We could tell that they wanted to play, so—using nothing but hand signals—we invited them in and selected teams. There were no rules. Nick and I had an eight-year-old goat herder on our team and the three eighteen-to-twenty-year-old herders were on the other team. This must have been the only time they had played basketball. They dribbled using two hands, stopped, dribbled again, passed, shot—all in bare feet.

The game was a rare experience. The goat herders were laughing as they handled the ball. When we passed the ball to the young goat herder, an ear-to-ear smile erupted on his face. When one of the older herders had possession, the young one, whom we had adopted into our team, did his best to tackle his opponent. The opposing team ran around the court, passing and bouncing until they put the ball up to the net. When we had the ball, the goat herders were like a moving obstacle course. We played basketball, of sorts, among the goats, goat droppings, and goat herders for an hour. It was a game of note, one that I will always remember. We left the court just before dark with pats on the back and only sign language to say goodbye.

After four months, phones were finally installed in our flat. This came about so quickly because we, as foreigners, were able to take advantage of a special phone expediting scheme the government had concocted to attract foreign investment. The occasion was worth celebrating. When it finally came down to the last three or four steps to get this phone activated, things got a bit complex. One day someone from the telephone department appeared at our door with two phones. He left the phones, with promises that another fellow would return later to hook them up. Later meant two weeks. When the technician finally arrived, he hard wired the two phones into the line and said that the phones would be activated. We would receive a call from the telephone department informing us of the phone numbers.

After four days without hearing a thing, we sent Selvan to the telephone office to find out what the obstacle was. He came back with the number for one phone and a promise that it would be activated within 48 business hours. Someone would call us. No calls. No calls. We started listening into the phones several times a day to see if they were working yet. On Sunday we heard an excited yell from our eldest son, Nick. He heard a dial tone on one line! The other was still dead. The curious thing was that the working phone line was not the one we had the number for. For the next three days we could dial out but had no indication of a phone number at which we could be reached. One more catch—while the phone was hooked up, the feature allowing long distance calls was not activated. Selvan made another trip to the telephone office. While he was there the telephone department activated the second line and provided Selvan with the phone number.

We thought our problems were over. When making the original hook-ups, however, the telephone company would only hardwire the phones. This meant that there was not a clip-in connector available for the fax machine or the computer modem. Two electrical companies later, along with a mere cost of 1,500 rupees, we had wires connected, one phone in the bedroom and one in the office, a fax machine hooked up, and modem capabilities. Hallelujah!

It wasn't ten minutes after the phones were finally sorted out that a call came in from my office in Michigan. Three minutes later the second phone rang with another person from the office on the line. Having a working phone in each hand was a marvel taken for granted in Michigan! The skinny green lizard crawled out of the clay pot in the corner of the room. Setting down one of the phones, I reached for the broom.

5

Hinduism
India's Ancient Religion
by Lakshmi Srinivas

"Whatever path he follows, every Hindu is aware of the difficulty, even the improbability, of reaching the ideal state in a single lifetime."

—Sudhir Kakar,
from *The Inner World*

"Death is with them a very frequent subject of discourse. They regard this life as, so to speak, the time when the child within the womb becomes mature, and death as a birth into a real and happy life for the votaries of philosophy."

—Megasthanes, 300 BCE,
the Greek ambassador to the court of Chandragupta,
from *Ancient India as Described
by Megasthanes and Arrian*

The room was still dark when Srinivas rolled over and opened his eyes. He crawled from under the wool blanket. A pale glow was beginning to form in the sky to the east. Though the sun was not up yet, traces of its light were taking the edge off the darkness. Srinivas sat on his bed rubbing his palms. He looked down at his hands, which were reverently placed together, and quietly said a verse of prayer. Srinivas passed his palms over his closed eyes and face before looking at the framed picture of the god on the wall of his room. He folded his hands one more time before stepping out of bed.

Srinivas brushed his teeth. He walked quietly to the room where the main god idol was kept. Again, Srinivas chanted several verses before walking to the stove to pour his first cup of coffee. Srinivas turned on the water in the shower and continued to get ready for the morning. He again stepped into the god's room, this time to light the oil lamp and the incense sticks. Srinivas recited more verses in prayer and prostrated himself before the idol. Srinivas was ready for breakfast.

Anita, his wife, Rishi, their son, and Rashmi, their daughter, joined in a similar ritual as their days began. Prayer was offered when the oil lamp was still glowing. Custom dictated that the oil lamp before the god's image, the idol, be lit once in the morning, earlier than noon, and again at dusk. While either Anita or Srinivas could light the oil lamp in the morning, at dusk, Anita, the lady of the house, was responsible for the task.

Srinivas walked past a small shelf built into the wall and could recognize the picture of the god he had been named after, positioned neatly above the shelf's surface. A small rope of flowers still draped over the picture's frame from the evening before, spreading the familiar smell of jasmine into the small room.

Lifting the latch on the door, Srinivas slipped into the narrow street. As he listened to the chatter of traffic in the neighborhood and breathed in the new morning air, he wondered whether he should walk to the temple before going to his office or take an auto-rickshaw. Srinivas stepped off the broken curb and took a few steps toward the corner. Today he would walk.

In India one can find multiple dimensions in multiple layers. One such dimension is religion. Of all the aspects of life in India, religion has a predominant position. Religion is a way of life in India. Swami Vivekananda, the great Indian thinker said, "Religion is a constitutional necessity for man and plays a role mightier than anything else in our life." Religion has been one of the most powerful factors in the creation and propagation of civilization and culture. It has influenced all that is beautiful and sublime in sculpture, painting, and other fine arts. India's rich religious culture has resulted today in a cosmopolitan array of religions including Hinduism, Buddhism, Christianity, Islam, Jainism, Sikhism, and Zoroastrianism.

A number of philosophical similarities exist between religions. Major religions, more or less, agree on the basic philosophy of good and evil. The inner experience a Hindu has while holding communion with God does not differ in essentials from the experience that a Muslim or a Christian has. But the three differ greatly in their mythologies and rituals. Religion is a heritage and a tradition. Every religion has theology and rituals that act as props or guides for the common person.

Religion in India has a multiplicity of local cults, beliefs and superstitions, and many village gods. Hinduism, Buddhism, Jainism, and Sikhism owe their origin and development to India. All of them bear the hallmark of the Indian spirit, or psyche.

Buddhism, Jainism, and Sikhism all appeared as reform movements within Hinduism. They were, in their inception, protests against the decadent and degenerate condition of Hinduism at the time. The founders of the three reform movements, Gautama Buddha (Buddhism), Vardhaman Mahavira (Jainism), and Guru Nanak

(Sikhism), each saw that the prevailing Hinduism was steadily deteriorating and established an alternative with practical attractions.

It would not be easy to understand India without understanding Hinduism because the life of a large section of her population is centered in this religion. So vital has been the role played by it in the development of India's character that Swami Vivekananda observed, "India lives so long as Hinduism lives." Mrs. Annie Besant also cherished a similar conviction. Addressing the students of the Hindu College, she once observed, "Make no mistake. Without Hinduism India has no future. Hinduism is the soil into which Indian roots are struck and torn out of that she would inevitably wither as a tree torn out from its place."

In its philosophy, Hinduism has allowed its followers to strike new paths. This has led to a large number of systems in the Hindu philosophy and a large number of sects within the fold of Hinduism.

Spiritual beliefs and doctrines that provide a bond of unity among Hindus are propounded in the various Hindu scriptures. Thus, the Hindu scriptures can be properly regarded as an important source of the unity that underlies Hinduism, and to some extent, India itself. Hinduism is ethnic in character; its growth and development are closely connected with the contemporary history of the races that came to India and settled over time. It is not built on Canon or Gospel. Hinduism is not articulated by the teachings of its founder. It is not an event-based historical religion, *per se*, like Buddhism, Islam, and Christianity. The teachings of the Hindu scriptures were formulated over the course of time and are now written in the four Vedas: Rig Veda, Yajur Veda, Sama Veda, and Atharvana Veda.

Hinduism, though based essentially on the teachings of the Vedas, is secondarily derived from the moral and religious precepts of prophets, saints, philosophers, and lawgivers of ancient, medieval, and modern times. Thus, Hinduism is a growing organism, constantly enriched by new insights, emerging from the experiences of living men and women.

The Srimad Bhagavad Gita, Krishna's sermon to the warrior Arjuna, a divine revelation, has been far more influential in shaping and molding the thoughts and beliefs of Hindus than any other scripture. The Gita is a unique treasure house of spiritual love. It is at once a science of the Eternal and a scripture of yoga. This combination is not to be found easily elsewhere.

According to Hinduism, religion is experience. Hindu ethics prescribe the disciplines for a spiritual life, which are to be observed consciously or unconsciously as long as a person lives. Hinduism speaks of universal ethical principles that apply to all human beings regardless of position in society or stage in life. As practiced in daily life by the average Hindu, religion is expressed with the worship of images and with symbolism, music, dancing, processions, prayer, feasting, and fasting. The lighting of a pair of oil lamps before the image of God after morning and before evening is a daily ritual both at home and in the temple.

The deities of popular Hinduism are symbols of the personal god. Their images are seen in temples and shrines. Popular worship in India is generally accompanied by a spirit of joyousness and merriment. The atmosphere of the temple reverberates with songs, hymns, and shouts of mirth.

There are male and female humanized gods. Brahma, *the creator*, Vishnu, *the protector*, and Shiva, *the destroyer,* are the most important male deities. Rama, Krishna, and Narasimha (face of a lion and body of a man) are some of the divine incarnations of Vishnu worshipped by the Hindus; Kartikeya, son of the divine mother Parvathi (consort of Shiva), and the embodiment of valor, is highly venerated in south India. Besides these, there are other male deities, such as Ganesha, the god with the elephant head who is the god of wisdom, and Hanuman, the monkey chieftain. Female deities include Lakshmi, the goddess of wealth, and Saraswathi, the goddess of learning. Kali and Durga represent Shakti, or creative power. Indra is the god of rain; Varuna, the god of water; Vayu, the god of air; Agni, the god of fire; and Surya (or Sun), the god of light. Each one of these gods and goddesses attracts dedicated worshippers. Different deities embody the diverse attributes and powers of the spirit. Worship may be offered to any of the symbols.

Hindus do not regard these gods and goddesses as independent entities or powers but look upon them as different manifestations of one and the same supreme spirit. The Upanishads unequivocally declare there is but one God. People call Him by different names.

Rituals help to create a religious climate. Though rituals, gods, and goddesses differ throughout India, there are underlying similarities. Images are worshipped in houses and also in temples. The deity is treated as an honored guest in the home, and in the temple as the king of kings. This is, in short, the popular religion practiced by a pious Hindu.

In temples, priests attend on the deity as on a king. Early in the morning the priest arouses the deity from sleep with music and, after giving him a ceremonial bath, dresses him in royal robes and decks him with ornaments and flowers. He waves light by lighting a piece of camphor before him and offers him food and drink. Then the deity holds court, giving audience to devotees, hearing their complaints, and granting their prayers. On festive occasions the deity is taken in procession with all the regalia befitting an emperor.

Through all these rituals and forms, the worshipper does not forget the absurdity of trying to gratify the spirit by means of perishable offerings. Festivals, fasts, birthdays of saints, and pilgrimages to holy places form a major part of the usual religious life of a Hindu.

Religious festivals are frequent in India. On these days, Hindus often observe fasts and offer special worships. Hindu mythology has stories of gods (Deva) winning battles over demons (Asuras), signifying the victory of good over evil. Many festivals commemorate events in Hindu mythology that symbolize the destruction of the forces of evil by those of good. A popular festival in north India, called the Ramlila, depicts the destruction by Rama of the wicked monster-king Ravana. So with the story of Deepavali, and the celebration signifies the Krishna's win over Narakasura.

Festivals are colorful occasions giving rise to innocent joys and merriments, offering relief from the routine chores of daily life. Fasting gives inner purity; the feasting that follows develops the social sense. Different days are set apart for different cults. Devotees often keep vigil for the whole night, reading from scriptures and worshipping. Special worship is offered on birthdays of the great religious teachers and mystics who were creators of India's spiritual culture. Pilgrimages are undertaken frequently by every practicing Hindu. The pilgrims, practicing austerity, often trek great distances into remote areas such as the Amarnath caves and Vaishno Devi in the northern-most Himalayan state of Jammu and Kashmir.

Hindu rituals and myths have enriched India's art, architecture, and literature. Temples, priests, and pilgrimages have kept Hinduism alive. Through religious festivals, pilgrimages, the observance of vows, and ritualistic worship, a Hindu cleanses the heart, renews contact with God, and makes progress toward a spiritual goal.

Hindus typically perform rituals at specific stages of life; birth, tonsure at age three, the beginning of education, initiation in the spiritual path at age eight, marriage, housewarming, and the sixtieth birthday. In some Hindu communities, the sixtieth birthday is considered rebirth. The Hindu calendar is made up of sixty years, each carrying a distinct name. The sixtieth birthday signifies completion of one round of the Hindu calendar.

Prominent Hindu festivals include Sankranti, also called Pongal in the Tamil Nadu region, or Bihu in Assam. Sankranti is normally celebrated on January 14th each year. Mahashivarathri is celebrated in February or early March. Holi, the festival of colors, celebrates the beginning of spring in late February or March. Next is the Lunar New Year (March/April), Ramanavami (April), the Solar New Year, also called Vishu in Kerala (April 14th), Raksha Bandhan/Upakarma (August), Krishna Janmashtami (August/September), Ganesh Chathurthi (August/September), Dasara (September/October), and Deepavali (November). The Hindu calendar is based on the lunar calendar, and dates of the Hindu festivals are not fixed relative to the traditional 365-day calendar.

Hindus attach significance to performing events at an auspicious time which are set in consultation with an astrologer. Horoscopes are a vital part of Hindu life. Birth is registered with a horoscope, making each person unique. Horoscope establishes the auspicious time for each important ritual in a person's life, such as the dates for marriage, housewarming (gruhapravesha), and the thread ceremony (upanayana). The position of the moon in the solar system at the time of birth according to the Hindu Lunar calendar determines the birthday of a person.

The distinguishing feature of the social organization of the Hindus is the caste system. According to the Hindu scriptures, a normal society consists of the Brahmins, people of knowledge, or science, literature, thought, and learning; the Kshatriyas, people of action and valor who were kings and rulers; the Vaishyas (business community), people of desires, possessiveness, and acquisitive enterprise; and the Sudras, simple people engaging mainly in manual labor. Each group has its own hygiene, its own domain of labor, its own sentiment of perfection, and its own special superiority.

In the Vedas, the four castes are described as four important parts of the body of the cosmic person: the head, the arms, the thighs, and the feet. The four castes are interdependent for the common welfare of all. Rules regarding the four castes are the product of many centuries of Hindu evolution.

The Hindu concept of marriage has unique attributes. Hinduism attaches a sanctity to the marriage tie that makes the union irrevocable. The Hindu marriage sacrament is viewed as the external and visible symbol of an inner and spiritual tie between the husband and the wife. In addition, many Hindus deem marriage to be the religious duty of every man and woman.

Traditionally, marriages were arranged from beginning to end by the parents of the bride and groom. In Hindu tradition, when a family had sons and daughters, the daughters were all married before the first son was married. And younger siblings married only after their elder ones had married. Parents of the son would choose the bride, and the son would unquestioningly marry. The bride and groom were strangers and were expected to abide by their parents' wishes. The prospective bride and groom would not meet before marriage. If they did, it would be before the elders in the family, in a common room, at the time of announcing the engagement.

Today, parents frequently allow their sons and daughters to meet a prospective spouse after the parents have 'short-listed' the candidates. The son's parents decide the selection of the prospective bride. In most cases, the son's parents are the ones with the final decision. As a prelude to an arranged marriage, the girl's parents approach the boy's parents with the horoscope of their daughter, along with information of family, their occupations, their property holdings, etc. If the boy's family is still interested in the girl, the boy's family gives the girl's horoscope to an astrologer, also known as *pandit,* who evaluates the suitability of the two horoscopes with each other. If the two tally on certain characteristics, the astrologer provides an approval to the boy's parents, who in turn ask the girl's family to set a meeting of the two families.

The families meet at the engagement ceremony hosted by the bride's family. An engagement ceremony is a formal announcement of the agreement of marital alliance. The astrologer sets the date and time of marriage, called the *Muhuratham* or auspicious hour, based on calculations from both the horoscopes of the couple.

In the past, the traditional marriage ceremony lasted four or five days and was hosted by the bride's family. Today the marriage ceremony is abridged and is usually complete in a day or two. The rituals performed at a Hindu marriage are elaborate, beginning several days before the actual marriage date and ending several days after.

The most striking feature of any Hindu marriage is the *kanyadaan,* which is the giving away of the daughter by her father in marriage to her husband, who takes a vow to keep her happy and take good care of her as his wife. This ritual is symbolic of the fact that the parents have actually washed their hands of their daughter. When a bride departs from her parental home and enters the home of her husband's family, her life is changed. She takes on new responsibilities, including lifelong duties in her new home, where she must share everything with her new family. She must fend for herself in her new home. Her parents do not interfere in her matters anymore.

In many Hindu castes, marriage vows are exchanged before a fire (*agni sakshi*). Many ritualistic functions take place in the presence of fire, which is considered most sacred. The rituals and duration of the marriage ceremony vary with each community among the Hindus.

Lunch on the marriage day is elaborate, often with as many as forty different items being served. The guests arrive in their best clothe, women in silk sarees, men in dhoti-kurta or pyjama-kurta, and children often in traditional Indian costumes.

The Hindu symbol of marriage is the *mangalsutra* made of gold in some communities, or gold and black beads in others. This is worn by the bride around the neck and is given to the bride by the groom during the marriage ceremony. This is the personal mark of marriage for the bride, and she wears it as long as her husband lives. Another symbol of marriage is the pair of silver toe-rings that a wife wears on the second toe of both feet. During the ceremony in most communities, the bride wears a vermilion at the roof of the forehead, called the *sindoor.*

The bride's trousseau has silk sarees, silver articles, utensils, gold and diamond jewelry, clothes, bed linens and other items of daily use—all that is required in a household.

The joint family is another Hindu social institution. In the joint family, the son does not set up a separate household after marriage but continues to live under the parental roof and share daily life with other members of the family.The undivided family becomes a large composite unit, including persons belonging to three, or even four, generations. Sometimes, the membership of a joint family may add up to nearly forty, including grandparents, granduncles and grandaunts, parents, uncles and aunts, married brothers and their children, cousins, nephews, and sometimes even great grandchildren. All of them live under the same roof, eat together, and hold property in common. The family unites in worship also. Like the caste system, the joint family is also found in other religious groups in the country. It is, however, primarily a Hindu social institution and has exercised profound influence upon the development of the Hindu way of life.

Common ownership of property in a joint family implies several things. It means that every son born into the family becomes a co-owner of the family property at the time of birth, and by virtue of birth. It means that no member keeps a separate purse. The earnings of all the members are pooled together and expenses of the family as a whole are met out of the common fund. Non-earning members have the same rights as earning members. All members of a joint family respect the authority of the head of the family, who is usually the eldest male in the line of male descent.

The joint family acts as a school in which a person learns to work for others in the spirit of selflessness. It teaches a small group of people, as no other institution can teach, how to live for the good of all. It develops the spirit of mutual helpfulness and of sacrifice for the sake of others. It guarantees at least a bare subsistence, the first condition of economic progress. The joint family affords a safe and respectable shelter to unfortunate widows. It enables its members to bridge periods of crisis and difficulties. Whether it is illness, enforced absence from home, or any other unforeseen calamity, one can always look to the joint family for support and sympathy. The joint family enables many older men to devote themselves to public service, since the responsibility for their wives and children can be met through family resources. The system preserves traditional customs and religious rites from generation to generation.

Hinduism is a way of life more than a creed, a process more than a result. It is subject to growth and change. Throughout its long history it has insisted on spiritual experience and fellowship, and not on conformity to a doctrine. It has often been characterized by absolute freedom of thought. It holds that truth, though absolute, has many phases and can be approached from different points of view. Accordingly, Hinduism has never laid claim to the exclusive possession of truth but has always admitted that different religions of the world embody different aspects of it.

6

Urban Jungle

"In a dramatic roundup, lines of beaters and kumkies drive an entire herd of wild elephants through the forest to a stockade. From this they are later taken to be tamed and trained—primarily to help in harvesting teak, rosewood, and other valuable timber...."

"...A trustee from the famous Hindu temple at Nagercoil, at the southernmost tip of the Indian peninsula, was shopping for young tuskers to serve as sacred elephants on ceremonial occasions. But the great majority of the elephants bought that day would find themselves in forest rather than temples."

—Harry Miller, "*Wild Elephant Roundup in India*" from *National Geographic,* March 1969

There were a number of elephants that lived in temples in Bangalore and periodically shifted from one location to another. When this happened, they blended in with traffic like any other vehicle. An elephant in traffic could have cars and motor scooters on all sides. A small mahout in a dhoti riding on the elephant's shoulders would give commands to the animal, much like a jockey to a horse. The elephant would often be carrying bags of rice or bundles of banana leaves on its back. It was a rare occasion when we saw more than one elephant in the city on the same day.

At intersections in Bangalore an elephant would pack into a crowd of bicycles, auto-rickshaws, cars, and trucks, fighting for its own position like everyone else. Cars inched up from behind, giving the occasional toot on the horn. Motor scooters wove through narrow separations between vehicles, shifting from one position to the next in an effort to get to their destinations. The entire street seemed to breathe like a living organism. As it exhaled, every vehicle shifted a little to find a better position. As the vehicles moved, the organism constricted with a massive inhale until each crevice filled with a vehicle that had shifted to occupy the available space and became part of a tight gridlock waiting for another small crack to appear, allowing another exhale to begin.

One motor scooter found itself tightly packed against the backside of the elephant, waiting to advance to a more favorable spot. As the traffic tightened around the scooter the elephant began to lift its tail. The scooter's driver looked up and frantically reached for the handlebars. He tried to pull the bike back but was trapped by a shiny white Ambassador. He leaned to the side but could tell he was not clear. He planted his feet and leaned back on the scooter seat. The elephant shifted its feet slightly, as if ready to back up. The driver jumped from the bike and grabbed for the bumper of the Ambassador.

Traffic exhaled—but not in time to change the fate of the scooter. As the elephant and other vehicles moved forward, the scooter driver reached down to gingerly pick up his dung-covered machine. Tenderly guiding it with only one finger of each hand, he made his way to the street side. In what seemed to be a giant inhale, the mass of sympathetic vehicles cramped together and parted, making a path for the scooter to exit from the rat race, acknowledging that it had paid its dues.

A more unusual event occurred when a herd of fifteen wild elephants made their way into a Bangalore suburb from Bannerghatta, a jungle reserve nearby. There were only fifteen wild elephants in a city of almost five million, but the pachyderms managed to create quite a commotion. They held the neighborhood at bay for nearly half a day, eating from the gardens and pushing things around until the police managed to frighten them back to their own habitat with a variety of noisemakers. It was a nice story for *The Deccan Herald* that day.

Perhaps the strangest creature I encountered on the streets of Bangalore approached me from a distance. I spotted it while out for an early-morning jog. The closer it got, the stranger it seemed. Was it a car? An animal? As it neared, I could tell it was an unusual combination of man and machine. There were actually three men, not themselves physically connected but linked by the full-size billboard that lay flat on their heads. This billboard was about four meters wide by eight meters long. One man was centered in the front. The other two each supported a rear corner. Each was riding a bicycle. All three pedaled and steered in unison, without hands on the sign, only balancing the sign on their heads. They moved in and out of traffic as if this arrangement was just another vehicle on the road. Equivalent to any other vehicle, they maneuvered around the monument in the center of the intersection. A lizard clinging to the side of the small obelisk watched them go by before darting into a crack in the pavement.

A distant relative of the billboard-bicycle was on the road in Delhi early one morning. It was easier to identify but no less exotic. In this case, a ten-meter bamboo ladder was being transported. The individual in front had managed to slip between the ladder's first and second rungs. The ladder was suspended off the ground at his waist. A similar man, though a bit huskier, had slipped into the last two rungs. Each man rode a separate bicycle. As they moved together, navigating around turns and from one lane to the next, they looked like a long fire truck with front and rear steering.

A floating creature caught my eye one morning while I was running around Ulsoor Lake. It was more of a raft than a boat but was unlike a traditional raft. The craft was made of thousands of discarded plastic bags, packed tightly into bales and held together with rope and wire. The bales were then tied to each other to make one large raft. This seagoing contraption seemed quite resourceful. Men fishing from it used a long pole to push from spot to spot. Their fishing gear consisted of sticks with strings tied to the end and seemed to be successfully catching blue gills for dinner.

Perhaps the most common creature that roamed the streets of Bangalore was a small crossbreed vehicle—the auto-rickshaw. An auto-rickshaw consisted of two main components, a small engine and a curled brass horn with a rubber squeeze ball on the end. One of the main responsibilities of the auto-rickshaw driver was to toot this horn at anything that crossed its path; or could cross its path; or might think about crossing its path; or perhaps just looked peculiar to the driver. An auto-rickshaw is a three-wheeled motor scooter with a canvas body intended to protect the passengers from the elements. Most of these vehicles had a pull-start lever, a taxi meter, a single hand-actuated windshield wiper, and an old shoe hanging from the rear axle. Pammi explained that the shoe was intended to ward off the evil eye.

Auto-rickshaws were commonly seen transporting everything from king-size mattresses to bathtubs. When we were having tile repaired in our flat, an auto-rickshaw delivered a full load of sand.

One day Selvan pulled our vehicle up to an intersection next to an auto-rickshaw that was carrying an amazing number of students. Ten children, all in uniform, were packed into the passenger compartment of the mighty vehicle, still leaving room for the driver. While marveling at this group, another auto-rickshaw pulled up behind it, holding four full grown men and three live sheep. While the two vehicles waited, a bicycle pulled up with a bundle of thirty chickens hanging by their feet from the handlebars. It was a sorry sight, all those dead chickens. I turned my head to get a closer look. The chicken I was looking at cocked its head to the right. I turned my head to the left. The chicken cocked its head to the left and stared into my eyes. I peered closely and realized that all the chickens were looking around a bit. Thirty *live* chickens on a bicycle. Now that was interesting.

Later in the week we saw another auto-rickshaw moving through traffic. This one was different because it had its seat cushion on the top of the canvas roof. Perhaps the driver left it there by mistake and started driving without knowing the cushion was on top. As we got closer it became apparent that the object was not a cushion, but was the back seat of the rickshaw, placed on top to make room in the back for floor-to-ceiling skinned mutton carcasses. Similar to the purpose of the chicken-bicycle, this open-air vehicle was making deliveries to butcher stands around the city, many of which were small open-air sheds, each with a dirt floor and a large tree stump used as a cutting surface.

Bicycles were seldom used for recreation in India. Most bicycles were simply the one-speed variety, with a leather seat and one hand-operated brake. The bicycle was one of the most practical forms of Indian transportation. Frequently walked beside rather than ridden, it was with much resourcefulness that this wheeled invention was converted into a transport device well beyond the vision of its originator. It was not unusual to see people carrying crates of eggs on a bicycle rack. The eggs were in something less than American egg crates, twenty-four per layer, twenty layers deep. The egg crates were strapped to the back rack with bungee cords. With the stack of crates taller than the rider, the bicycle moved through traffic, over potholes, starting, stopping, walking, and riding as if the eggs required no special consideration at all.

Eggs were also occasionally carried uncrated, in plastic bags of about 100, hanging from the handlebars. Frequently the bicycle carried stacks of egg crates over the rear wheel and bags of loose eggs suspended from the handlebars.

Motor scooters also had their cargo uses. Two men on a motor scooter carried the windshield of a full-size industrial truck. The passenger on the back held it vertically on edge, extending about two meters into the air. There was no special packaging.

Another motor scooter had a similar idea but with cargo that was less fragile. Two men transported a full-size mattress, which was standing on end, wedged between the driver and the passenger. With this huge sail the man on the back was doing everything he could to keep from being swept off as the scooter moved forward.

Public buses were also a treat. The designed seating capacity was about 45, but during peak hours, buses often carried more than 120 people. This included several layers of people hanging on to the side of the bus at the front and rear doors.

In Bangalore there were three styles of double-decker buses. The first, a traditional two-level bus, was simply a taller variety than a normal bus. In Bangalore, each bus of this type had massive dents at the leading top edge from hitting low-hanging tree branches and other obstacles. Another type of double-decker bus was similar to a trailer pulled by a cab, with the trailer constructed for two levels of passengers. The third type of double-decker was a single-level bus with people riding on top. The 'open air' upper compartment included nothing more than the roof and the luggage rack to hang on to. It increases the capacity of a full bus by about twenty people. Riding on top must have been reasonably safe and better than walking. There was the concern, however, about how the people on the top got along when the vehicle encountered the objects that put dents into the other double-deckers. Top riders were not normally city buses but those that brought groups of workers to and from a local village every day.

On the outskirts of Bangalore, there was a famous banyan tree. This was a large tree by any standards. The roots dropping to the ground from the branches enabled the single tree to span several acres. The roots eventually developed into a very complicated trunk system, and branches went on almost indefinitely. Not only did a tree like this become a terrific habitat for wild monkeys, snakes, and green lizards, it often became the home of a shrine, as did the Bangalore banyan tree, giving it almost sacred status. When we visited the tree, a small man emerged from the branches to provide a descriptive tour of it.

He followed one step behind us, and as we walked through the entanglement, he raised his arm to point and say with wonderful expression, "That is a branch!"

We walked a bit further and raising his hand again, he enthusiastically orated, "That is a branch!"

He continued with this phrase for the full two acres, until when we nearly returned to the beginning, he raised his arm, pointing to some movement in the limbs, and clearly announced, "Monkey!"

I handed him twenty rupees and thanked him for the tour. A lizard scampered into a hollow opening of one of the roots nearby.

From time to time while we were in Bangalore, there were political or social disruptions. The city government always feared volatile situations that could erupt quickly into an out-of-control mob. When events of this nature were on the horizon, the government would enact a bundh, closing down business, schools, and other normal activities. In Michigan, the children had snow days that closed the schools. In India, they had what we called riot days.

One week there was a bit of a riot in front of the Basavanagudi office. In this case, a group of local citizens had a misunderstanding regarding rubble that was being hauled away by the city while the city was drilling a bore well. A rumor spread throughout the community that the city had torn down a mosque and was hauling it away. This, in turn, started a fight between two religious factions, and then between everyone. There seemed to be a million people on the streets in front of the office. Four people were killed. The police opened fire on the crowd, which resulted in two of the deaths. A police inspector was also stabbed and died. A young couple in a car were chased and then crashed into a wall, killing the woman in the passenger seat. The event led to several days of curfews. Most schools were closed for two days. People at the office were trapped at work all day and night.

Not long after the riot, we had to replace the sign outside of our office to comply with a new state regulation. The regulation was a result of local protests by people from our state, Karnataka, who were upset about having English or Hindi on signs. Both English and Hindi were official national languages spanning all of India. The local language was Kannada, which was what the protesters wanted on the signs. The office sign was in English and Kannada, but our problem was that the English was on top, with Kannada below, an arrangement no longer allowed. Our new sign contained the same information but reversed the positions of the English and Kannada names.

It took some time for us to become accustomed to Indian names and places. Our first encounter with districts of the city like Koramangala and Basavanagudi took some practice. The names seemed so long and musical. Every day in the paper we could find a name more difficult for us to pronounce and read than what we had seen the day before. We began to look for record-breaking names. For instance, an article described how Mr. Veerahanumanthappa had assaulted Mr. Doddagangadhara. These were world-class names, names with a ring to them. In our office there was an individual whose business card sported the name Lakshminarasimhaiah. I liked this name. Although it would never make it through my computer's spell checker, it overflowed with character.

I suppose that just as many of the people we encountered while living in India had some difficulty recognizing, remembering, and pronouncing our American names. On one occasion Cathy went to the corner chemist (pharmacy) to buy vitamin C. The chemist slipped a package of tablets into a small homemade bag, constructed from neatly folded carbon copies of customer's receipts. He set the package on the counter and put an old piece of carbon paper between the next two pages of the receipt pad.

"Who is the medicine for, madam?"

"Dan," Cathy replied.

The chemist wrote the date and asked, "How is that spelled?"

"D." He looked up over his glasses and penciled the letter.

"A." He repeated the procedure.

"N." The chemist firmly wrote the letter "M" to complete the word Dam.

The chemist looked at what he had written and glanced over his glasses at Cathy.

"Is this right?"

Cathy inspected the word and responded, "No, actually it has an 'N' at the end".

The chemist carefully added the letter "N". "Thank you, madam. Have a pleasant day."

Cathy shrugged her shoulders, chuckled a bit and wondered who would get the bag made from the recycled Damn receipt.

As time went on, we noticed fewer of the small differences in daily life that had captured our curiosity from the beginning. We could look at the number

1,00,00,000 and forget that the commas were not positioned the way we were used to in Michigan. We could tell someone that there was a lakh of people in Cubbon Park, and the person would know that the crowd was 100,000 strong. A business associate could talk about a company with five crores of turnover, and we knew he meant fifty million rupees. And before long, we could move our heads from side-to-side, with the slightest figure eight to the movement, and our colleague knew that the side-to-side head movement meant "Yes."

7

Occasions of Note

"If all the year were playing holidays,
To sport would be as tedious as to work;
But when they seldom come, they wish'd for come,
And nothing pleaseth but rare accidents."

—William Shakespeare
from *King Henry the Fourth, Part I*

Most expatriates know that there are two sets of holidays; one celebrated where you are living, the other celebrated where you have come from. The first provides an exciting chance to meld into the local culture; the second brings a heartfelt longing to connect with and preserve one's own roots.

Thanksgiving was a holiday not celebrated in India. Those from the USA trying to carry on the tradition had somewhat limited choices. Turkeys were not common in Bangalore. When Thanksgiving arrived, we had settled on a couple of small chickens as a substitute. The American holiday fell on an Indian workday. When I arrived home from the office in the evening, Cathy met me at the front door and guided me to the kitchen to carve the meat. I reached into the oven and, much to my surprise, found a beautifully browned turkey cooked to perfection. Surprises like this were one of the pleasures of life as an expatriate. The turkey was nearly worth its weight in gold.

We had invited our neighbors to our flat for the feast. They brought a bottle of white wine that they had carried back from Singapore months earlier, as well as two homemade pumpkin pies. For a short time we could taste and smell the holiday that was so special in Michigan.

It wasn't until three days later that the real story came out regarding how this turkey was acquired. Cathy had called around town, asking other people in the international community where a turkey could be found in Bangalore. The trail finally led to a poultry shop with which we had some familiarity. Cathy contacted the store and arranged for the bird as a special order.

On Thanksgiving Day, Cathy arrived at the appointed time to pick up the turkey. "Come back in two hours, madam," the owner of the shop politely instructed.

After two hours Cathy returned. "Madam, your turkey has not yet arrived. You must come back in two more hours."

As Cathy arrived a third time, a thin man pulled up to the storefront on a bicycle with a plastic bag tied to the handlebars.

Cathy opened the door to the poultry shop. "Yes, madam, your turkey will be ready in just two minutes." The proud smile on the butcher's face indicated that he knew he had done well.

Cathy took the neatly wrapped package to the flat and began to open it at one end. Two turkey feet with claws flopped out of the paper and dangled over the counter's surface. Cathy looked away and pulled the tape off the other end of the package. The turkey's head flopped out, with small feathers peppering the nearly bald scalp. Cathy quickly taped the package together again and called Molly.

Christmas was also a challenge for those used to cutting a live pine tree for the season. There was a mad scramble by many expatriates around town in early December to find a suitable tree. No one divulged their source until the tree was found, paid for, and sitting in their living room with decorations. The lucky ones had shipped an artificial tree from home when their belongings were originally dispatched. We had not. It took us several tries to find something that would work.

Our first attempt was a live tropical fir tree that we bought with great excitement and expectation from the supply yard at Lalbagh Botanical Gardens. It was alive and green and had things that looked like needles. Beyond that, it was a closer cousin to carrot greens than to a pine tree. Once the ornaments were hung from the branches, the tree looked pathetic. The limbs on the top stuck straight out and were longer than the limbs on the bottom which drooped down pointing to the trunk. After looking at this creation for half a day, we finally had to undecorate it and return it to the outdoors.

Our next mission was to scour the city to find an artificial tree that looked like it grew in the woods of Michigan, or perhaps in New York City, or at least somewhere where a pine tree could grow! We would even have been happy with something that looked like it came from a department store window. Once again Cathy combed the alleys of the city until she came up with an honest-to-goodness artificial Christmas tree. All was well.

An interesting story was told by Nick's school friend from London whose family was elated to have found a real (cut) Christmas tree in Bangalore. The tree had been spray-painted green, which was not so unusual to us since most of the ones sold in Michigan have had the same treatment. The interesting side to this tree was that when the family dragged it into their house, it left a trail of

71

branches as they went. When they looked more closely, they discovered that most of the branches on the tree didn't originally belong to the tree. The trunk was expertly drilled with holes and at least fifty percent of the branches were simply stuck into the holes to make the tree look naturally full. Some entrepreneur had made one good, thick tree out of two or three sparse ones. It seemed to work.

Our neighbors had a boy, Glen, who was the same age as Kirk, our youngest son. The two often played together in the courtyard and did things together when both families were on outings. During our stay, Glen spent a lot of time preparing to accept his first communion in the Catholic Church. A large celebration was arranged at Glen's grandmother's bungalow near Ulsoor Lake. It was an outdoor party in the evening with many adults, children, friends, relatives, and business associates.

Cathy and I stood under one of the trees in the yard, surveying the setting and watching darkness descend on the scene. The yard was decorated with festive lanterns. Bouquets of balloons were floating above each table. A buffet of roast pig and other delicacies bordered the walkway into the bungalow. On each table a candle was burning, casting a warm glow of light on the small groups of people sitting close by.

The event was great for socializing. Adults bunched together at various tables set up around the lawn. Glen, Kirk, and five other young boys were sitting around their own table, just trying to be cool. This was definitely a boys' club. They looked like miniature grown-ups, each wearing a suit and tie, but there was also something mischievous about the group.

The evening went on. Cathy and I collected plates of food and found friends to sit with while we ate. The boys continued their discussion in the corner of the yard. They sat at the round table, hovering over the dim candle as if discussing a secret strategy of great importance.

Without warning, a considerable explosion erupted from the corner of the yard where the boys had been sitting. The concussion blew boys to the ground in a circle around the table. One by one, they stood up to brush the dust off their jackets. Each boy had a look of guilt and shock on his face.

No one said a word to his parents. They did, however, spend some time trying to sort things out among themselves.

Later, at home, Kirk explained the situation: "One boy thought it would be cool to set the string of the balloon at the table on fire—like a fuse." There was the candle and the string. What a temptation. It was an interesting way to learn that balloons in India are frequently filled with carbide gas rather than helium. Fortunately, all the boys walked away with only singed hair, lost eyebrows, slight facial burns, and a healthy respect for balloons.

There are many holiday festivals in India. Some are regional, others are national. Nearly all are connected to Hinduism, Islam, or Christianity. Many times, we knew something about a holiday before it arrived. Often, we found out accidentally.

The Ganesh festival is a two-week occasion honoring one of Hinduism's most important deities. Ganesh has the body of a heavy-set man and the head of an elephant. During this festival families and businesses displayed statues of Ganesh in front of their homes or buildings. It is an auspicious time. We knew the festival was going on but were surprised one morning when we went for a morning run around Ulsoor lake and watched as families and businesses, with great celebration, took their statues to the lake to throw them into the drink. As we ran by, a company backed its stake truck up to the bank and launched a three-meter-tall plaster Ganesh into the water. The group marked the occasion with lots of noise making, chanting, drum banging, and colorful flowers. Meanwhile another group with a large statue of Ganesh waited in line with their wooden-wheeled cart, pulled by two beige bulls that were colorfully decorated and that had bells on the ends of their horns. The queue was already long. How many of these Ganesh statues were at the bottom of the tank after untold years of celebration?

Deepavali, one of India's most important festivals, is known as the festival of lights. While, traditionally, oil lamps were lit after dark in homes, much of the original lighting has been eclipsed by electric lights strung all over the city. Most of the population is given two days leave from work. Many families in India spend the time visiting each other and exchanging sweets. A favorite activity during Deepavali was igniting a variety of explosives. The noise went on day and night for nearly a week until the festival was over. It carried on well beyond that for those who were really in a festive mood! The fireworks ranged from sparklers to dynamite—all day and all night long. On the first night of Deepavali, our neighbors made a fire in the courtyard, topping it off from time to time by tossing in an explosive equivalent to a quarter stick of dynamite. The ritual escalated for three days, at which time the city was so smoky from gunpowder that we could hardly see across the street.

One Deepavali morning *The Deccan Herald* informed us that Bangalore's electrical supply warehouse had gone up in smoke when a stray rocket found its way into the building's ventilation system. The building and its contents were a complete loss. It was just one more setback for an electrical system that was chronically crippled.

Holi is India's holiday known for fun. Although celebrated more aggressively in northern India where there is a distinct end to the winter season, we did see our share of the festivities in Bangalore. This was the festival of color. In fact, anyone on the street became a target for a splash of iridescent powder. People showed up at the office, having been pelted with packets of orange, red, and blue. Cattle roaming the streets or bulls pulling carts temporarily displayed a collage of bright paint splashes to augment the brass tips that ornamented the tips of their horns. It was as if the city turned into a huge game of paint ball. Those who had been hit wore their color like a medal, an acknowledgment that they had been the object of some special attention.

Dasara, a ten-day festival in autumn, is another of the most celebrated Hindu holidays. It was of particular importance in Mysore, not far from Bangalore, where southern India's famous Dasara procession takes place. During the afternoon of the last day of the festival, a lengthy parade of ornately decorated elephants and people in traditional Mysore dress began the royal procession, following a route from the Mysore Palace to Bannimantap in Mysore. At Bannimantap, there is a tree called the Banni tree to which the kings of Mysore offered prayers on this auspicious day. During the days of kingship, there was also a return procession, which has since been discontinued. Much like Deepavali, Dasara is celebrated with fireworks and exuberance, from beginning to end.

Frequently, festivals were accompanied by pujas (ceremonies) at temples, businesses, and homes. In a business, a Hindu holy man would perform a ceremony to bless the facility, bless the equipment, or bless the business itself. When beginning a venture, occupying a new home, erecting a new building, or approaching any other milestone, the timing of the event was always carefully considered, and an auspicious time was selected. Important milestones were frequently blessed by performing a puja, intended to make the enterprise trouble-free and promote a successful endeavor.

One morning we made our way to the basement of our apartment and found Selvan standing next to the Tata Estate, which had been decorated with colorful streamers, banana leaves, and flowers. Selvan indicated that there were some formalities we must take care of before he could drive for the day. He handed me a coconut and instructed me to crack it on the ground. He placed a plate with uncooked rice, a coin, a banana, and some incense on the ground near the vehicle. Selvan positioned a small lime under each tire. He started the engine and pulled forward, flattening each fruit as the car moved.

Turning sharply in the parking area, Selvan pulled the Tata Estate around and opened the doors for each of us to board. With a broad smile on his face, he drove out of the garage and began the daily routine. He looked as if a load had been lifted from his shoulders. A green lizard clung to the white wall as we drove up the ramp into the daylight.

8

Mughal Times

by Lakshmi Srinivas

"After viewing this monument of an Emperor, whose great actions have resounded throughout the world, and whose liberality and humanity were his highest praise, I became desirous of seeing even that stone which contained his crumbling remains. There was an old Mollah who attended, and had the keys of the interior building, (which is still held in veneration) and who obtains a precarious subsistence by shewing it to the curious traveler. Inside of the tomb is a vast hall, occupying the whole space of the interior of the building, which terminates in a dome; a few windows at the top admit a "dim religious" light, and the whole is lined with white marble. In the center the body is deposited in a sarcophagus of plain white marble, on which is written, in inlaid black marble, simply the name of ACBAR."

—William Hodges, 1793,
from *Travels in India During the Years 1780, 1781, 1782, 1783*

The feudal period in India from about 700 CE to 1500 CE was dominated by the spread of Islam throughout the north. Repeated political conquests by invading Persian and Arabian forces resulted in an integration of race, culture, religion, and political style. The conquest of Muhammad of Ghur from 1173 CE to 1206 CE to unify much of northern India forced the mass conversion of the populace to Islam. After Muhammad's death, the empire fragmented and reunified, to varying degrees, numerous times under the control of Islamic rulers, setting a framework for the Mughal period.

Mughal dynastic rule began with Babar, a descendant of Genghis Khan and Timur, the great Central Asian empire builders. Babar was the ruler of a small state in Central Asia. In 1526, at the request of a group of dissatisfied Afghan nobles, Babar defeated Ibrahim Lodhi, the ruler of Delhi, at Panipat and established Mughal rule in India, with Agra as the imperial capital.

Babar is known for the beautiful gardens with running water, cascading fountains, and marble pavilions laid out under his rule. Similar gardens were developed in many Mughal monuments. Babar was greatly attracted by the gear-and-chain water-lift device, to which Anglo-Indian usage later gave the name of the "Persian wheel." Babar is said to have first seen this device at Bhera in West Punjab in 1519.

After his death in 1530, Babar was succeeded by his son Humayun. Humayun initially was unable to retain power and was soon defeated by Sher Shah, an Afghan ruler. Humayun fled, taking refuge in Iran. In 1554, he returned to India and conquered his lost empire. Soon after, Humayun died as a result of a fatal fall down the steps to his library. Humayun's tomb in Delhi has become a landmark of the city.

His teenaged son, Akbar, ascended the throne in 1556. Though only thirteen years of age when he became Emperor, Akbar became one of the greatest rulers of the country and reigned for forty-nine years. He was an able administrator who introduced efficient infrastructure throughout his empire. Akbar was receptive to all the religions of the region: Islam, Hinduism,

Jainism, and Sikhism. He had several wives, among them a lady of the Hindu royal family of northwestern India: Jodha Bai. Akbar established his own eclectic religion, Din-I-lahi, whose followers were from all religions. This religion, however, disappeared soon after Akbar's death.

It was during Akbar's time that Sikhism, the socio-religious community founded by Guru Nanak, became prominent. Like offspring, many new religious movements are born out of and shaped by existing faiths. They bear likeness to the parents. Sikhism was born out of a wedlock between Hinduism and Islam.

The story of the Sikhs is the tale of the rise, fulfillment, and collapse of Punjabi nationalism. It begins in the latter part of the 15th century with Guru Nanak initiating a religious movement emphasizing what was common between Hinduism and Islam and preaching the unity of these two faiths practiced in Punjab. By the beginning of the 17th century, the movement crystallized with the formation of a third religious community consisting of the disciples, or *sikhas,* of Nanak, and the succeeding teachers, or *gurus.* Its mysticism found expression in the anthology of their sacred writings, the *Adi Granth,* comprising the writings of the Sikh gurus, as well as those of Hindu and Muslim saints.

Nanak was a strict monotheist. He refused to accept any compromise on the concept of the unity of God. A good Sikh, therefore, must not only believe that God is the only one, omnipotent, and omniscient being, but also conduct himself in such a way towards his fellow beings as does not harm them. Hurtful conduct, like lying, cheating, fornication, trespassing on others' property, does not conform to the truth that is God. This principle is stated categorically by Nanak in the opening lines of his most celebrated morning prayer, the *Japji,* and is the *mul mantra,* or the basic belief of Sikhism.

Guru Nanak rejected much that the Hindus of those days accepted as inseparable from Hinduism: for example, the caste system, idol-worship, *shraddha* (rites performed after death), belief in a dip in the holy Ganges as having a purification effect, and fasting. He sought to bring the Hindus and the Muslims closer to each other by eliminating the narrowness of outlook that characterized both and laying emphasis on the worship of one god common to both In this way, he introduced a new approach to religious feeling.

Sikhism of the first five gurus and the *Granth* found ready acceptance among the masses. They responded to it because it was eclectic, simple, and preached by men who were too modest either to claim kinship with god or to clothe their utterances in the garb of prophecy. What they wrote or said had a familiar ring in the people's ear. The Hindus caught the wisdom of the Vedas, of which the common people knew but little because of the monopoly over Sanskrit learning maintained by the Brahmins. The Muslims were reminded of the exhortations of the Sufis. To both the Hindus and the Muslims, the message of the gurus came in a language they understood. Although this kept Sikhism from those who could not understand Punjabi, within the Punjab, its appeal was irresistible. It had all the elements of a national faith, and until it crystallized into a distinct sect with a political purpose, it continued to excite the admiration of all Punjabis.

Like Buddhism, Sikhism is against the use of Sanskrit for religious purposes. Guru Nanak and the succeeding nine gurus composed their songs and hymns in the regional Punjabi language. The use of the regional language and of *Gurumukhi,* a new script, greatly helped Sikhism develop as an independent religion. It also

80

proved to be a serious obstacle in the way of its developing into an all-India religion.

In the early stages of the movement under Guru Nanak, Muslims were favorably disposed towards Sikhism. Akbar's tolerance for many religions must have contributed to this. Sikhism's belief in one God and its opposition to idolatry and the caste system, its condemnation of empty rituals, and its emphasis on equality and the congregation of humanity greatly appealed to Muslims. As a result, for a short period of time Sikhism slowed down the process of Islamic conversion of Hindus, which had been going on unobstructed for hundreds of years. When finally free to choose a religion, many low-caste Hindu converts had embraced Islam not because they were convinced of its superiority, but because of the prospects that it offered to improve social status. Sikhism was an alternative to Islam, the religion forced on them by conquers, and though similar to Hinduism, the religion of their heritage, it allowed better social status than Hinduism. Because of the large number of new converts, orthodox Muslims eventually sought the intervention of Akbar to halt the spread of Sikhism. Akbar paid no heed to their complaints.

What Varanasi was to the Hindus and Mecca to the Muslims, Amritsar became to the Sikhs—their most important place of pilgrimage. In 1604, the work on the Golden Temple at Amritsar was completed and the *Granth* Sahib, the holy volume, was formally installed in the temple at Amritsar. The *Granth* reflected the faith of Nanak in its entirety. Its hymns were of a high poetic order, its language intelligible to the illiterate peasant, its ethics simple and direct. The *Granth* became the most powerful factor in spreading the teachings of the gurus among the masses.

Mughal architecture is distinctive throughout India. In addition to forts, Mughals erected palaces, tombs, and mosques, that were an architectural blend of Persian patterns and an indigenous genius for fine craftsmanship. Akbar, in 1565, ordered the construction of a fort beside the Yamuna River in what is now called Agra. The imposing Agra Fort, built of red sandstone.

Akbar had power, prestige, and great wealth in the prime of his youth; he also had a number of wives, but no heir. A mystic, Salim Chisti, prophesied that the emperor would have not one but three sons. When the prophecy came true, Akbar built a new capital city, Fatehpur Sikri, with residential palaces on the rocky ridge outside Agra where Salim Chisti had his dwelling. Fatehpur Sikri consists of a number of highly unique structures in red sandstone with intricate ornamentation. An enormous congregational mosque, the Jami Masjid, was erected at the summit of the ridge. A massive triumphal gate, the Buland Darwaza, the biggest gateway in south Asia, marks the southern entrance to the mosque. The complex also houses the single story decorated tomb of Salim Chisti.

Akbar's own palace was a double story structure. Spectacular accompanying buildings include the Turkish Sultana Begum's palace, the Diwan-i-khas (the Hall of Private Audience), the enthralling Panch Mahal, the Hawa Mahal, Mariam's palace, and Birbal's house. Akbar's buildings at Fatehpur Sikri bear testimony to his magnificence. They are an impressive blending of Indian and Saracenic styles.

The practice of rulers meeting the public in a fixed venue so that appeals could be presented was introduced by Akbar. This also acted as a forum where other public displays could take place, such as the presentation of distinctions to officers of the king, the public reception of distinguished guests, the review and inspection of animals of the state, and furious elephant fights.

Akbar had a keen interest in technology and promoted the development and use of scientific concepts. The Persian wheel invention, which had been used earlier by Babar, was extensively employed at Fatehpur Sikri to enable water to be lifted to great heights through successive mechanical devices. In 1826, while the city lay in ruin, Heber observed: "The whole hill on which the palace stands bears marks of terraces and gardens, to irrigate which an elaborate succession of wells, cisterns and wheels appears to have been contrived adjoining the great mosque and forcing up the water nearly to the height of its roof. The cisterns are still useful as receptacles of rainwater, but the machinery is long since gone to decay" (Habib, p.137).

Abul Fazl, the biographer appointed by Akbar, includes chapters in Akbar's biography about assessing the purity of gold in all its various grades, extraction of gold, silver, and copper from the ore and their purification, extraction of perfumes, the making of soap, and the cooling of water by the use of saltpeter. The biography also describes how in order to overcome India's "absence of cold water and the excess of heat," Akbar popularized the use of khas-frames. "There is a fragrant root, very cool, which is called khas. By His Majesty's command, it became common to make huts of bamboo frames stuffed with it. When water is thrown on it, winter seems to arrive in the midst of summer" (Habib, p.134).

Akbar was interested in textile technology. "His Majesty has such an eye for the finer things that he has introduced silken clothes, brocade, tapestry and carpets of silk and brocade in India, and instructed highly skilled masters in that art, so that the work in India is now much better than the work of Persia and Europe" (Habib, p.132).

The manufacture of boats and ocean-going ships was highly advanced during the Mughal period, perhaps in some ways more advanced than British technology. Many ships were employed in foreign trade. They visited ports of the Persian Gulf, East Africa and South-East Asia.

Abul Fazl describes the construction of the first great ship by the side of River Ravi at Lahore. When it was completed in 1594, Emperor Akbar went to see it being launched. A thousand persons drew the ship with various ingenious devices, but it took ten days to put it into the river. It was difficult to find enough water in the Ravi to accommodate a seagoing vessel. Finally, it reached Bandar Lahiri, the seaport.

Akbar, though a mighty emperor, had to buy passes from the Portuguese for sea-travel from the Indian ports to the gulf for trade and also for pilgrimages. The Portuguese established themselves firmly by setting up fortresses and factories on the western coast of India by 1556, when Akbar ascended the throne. The Portuguese restricted navigation in the Indian Ocean by enforcing passes on the merchants, the nobility, and the rulers of the subcontinent. Portuguese officials issued passes against a nominal payment and the ships had to return to the stipulated port for the payment of custom duties. Those who did not abide by the terms and conditions of the passes risked confiscation of their vessels and cargo.

Mathematics and astronomy developed greatly during Akbar's reign. The famous Indian textbook on mathematics, *Bhaskara's Lilavati*, was translated into Persian at Akbar's court. Persian was the language of the court, and Arabic was studied by the learned. Works from Sanskrit were translated into Persian and from Arabic into Sanskrit. At the same time, encyclopedic works containing accounts of many sciences were translated from Sanskrit into Persian and from Persian and Arabic into the Indian languages.

Akbar died in 1605. His tomb was constructed at Sikandra, near Agra.

Akbar was succeeded by his son, Jahangir, who ruled from 1605 to 1627 and who was successful in further expanding the Mughal empire. The emperor was the source and spring of justice, not only because he heard and decided civil and criminal cases, but also because he was the protector of the poor and the oppressed. Jahangir constructed a chain of gold, thirty yards in length, containing sixty bells. It was fastened at one end to the battlements of the Shah Burj in the Agra Fort and at the other to a stone post on the bank of the River Yamuna. Any injured person who failed to obtain justice from the courts could come to shake the chain and, by ringing the bells, give notice to the wrong. Jahangir held a tribunal once every week to hear civil and criminal cases.

Jahangir, however, did not have his father's tolerance toward Sikhism. Shortly after Akbar's death, Guru Arjun, an important Sikh saint, was put to death. His execution was a profound shock to the people. Jahangir ordered the arrest of the guru's family and confiscation of his property. Local officials would not carry out the directive, believing that the death of the guru alone would subdue the Sikhs for a long time. The result was just the opposite. Arjun's son, Hargobind, after taking over the seat of his father, took to arms to avenge his father's killing.

As is the case in Indian life today, astrology played an important role in Mughal times. Seven comets appeared between 1526 and 1707 during the rule of the Mughals. There is one description detailing the fall of a meteorite. Jahangir, in his memoirs, records that on April 19, 1621, in one of the villages of the district of Jalandhar in Punjab, a frightful commotion occurred, and such a terrible noise came from the east that the residents of the village were shaken with fear. A light appeared falling from the heavens as if there was a rain-shower of fire from the sky. When people regained their senses, a rapid messenger was sent to the Amil (revenue collector) of the district, Muhammad Said, who at once rode on horseback to the village. He found that ten-meters by twelve-meters of ground had burnt so intensely that no sign of vegetation remained, and the earth was still hot. He had the ground dug out. The deeper they dug the greater was the heat; then they found a piece of burning red-hot iron so hot that it seemed to have come from a 'sphere of fire'. After some time it cooled down and was sent to the emperor in a sealed packet. Jahangir found that its weight was 160 *tolas* (about 2 kilograms).

Jahangir handed the meteorite to his master smith, Daud, for making a sword, a dagger, and a knife. He was informed that it was too brittle for hammering and would go to pieces, so the emperor ordered it to be mixed with ordinary iron. By mixing three parts of the meteorite, or *lightning iron*, with one part of other iron, two swords, one dagger, and a knife were made. Jahangir said that the swords were as good as those of Yemen and of 'the South' (Deccan) and were sufficiently flexible to bend and regain form. He had them tested in his own presence and found them to match well with the best swords. He named one of them "Cutting Sword" and the other "Lightning-Like". A poet composed a quatrain about them emphasizing their celestial origin: "Out of lightning fell raw iron in his reign" (Habib, p.116).

Superstitions related to eclipses influenced Jahangir so greatly that he described them in his memoirs. The total lunar eclipse of January 20, 1609 inspired Jahangir to weigh himself against gold, silver, cloth, and grain. He gave these and other things as alms to ward off the evil effect of the eclipse. About the solar eclipse of December 1610, Jahangir gives no details, except to tell us that to ward off the evil influences he again weighed himself against precious metals and gave away these and other articles and animals (horses, elephants, and bullocks) in alms at Agra and at other places. During the eclipse of March 1615, precious metals, animals, and cereals were distributed among the needy and the deserving.

Jahangir was followed by his son, Shah Jahan. Shah Jahan is known most for creating the Taj Mahal, one of the architectural feats of the world. It took twenty-two years and over 20,000 persons to erect the Taj Mahal. Shah Jahan outdid his predecessors in the magnificence of his court. He used marble in constructing most of the buildings of his time.

The Taj Mahal was the last and greatest work of architecture of the Mughal period in Agra, before Shah Jahan shifted the imperial capital to Shahjahanabad, today's Delhi, in 1639. Describing the new capital of the Mughal Empire, Chandar Bhan Brahman, a noble in the emperor's court wrote in 1648, "its towers are the resting place of the sun... its avenues are so full of pleasure that its lanes are like the roads of paradise. Its climate is beautiful and pleasant ..." (Blake, p. xi). The new city, built between 1639 and 1648, sprawled along the banks of the River Yamuna in the southeastern sector of the Delhi triangle. The cityscapes of Shahjahanabad were dominated by the palaces and mansions of the emperors and their nobles. The imperial city was the model for the empire.

Shah Jahan was a strict administrator who is also known to have ensured impartial judgment. This period of Mughal rule was said to be "rich beyond compare, and undisturbed by foreign aggression." Jahangir and Shah Jahan were great patrons of art, and a new style of painting, the Mughal school, developed. The Mughal school, with its distinct style, shows the imprint of the Safavid and Timurid art traditions and some influence of the classical Indian schools, particularly in manuscript painting. In Mughal paintings only the key figures of an event appear in the scene, and the whole action revolves around them.

Eight years before his death, the emperor was deposed by his son, Aurangzeb, and imprisoned in the Agra Fort. During his imprisonment, he had a view of the Taj Mahal, the tomb of his second wife, Mumtaz Mahal. Shah Jahan was finally laid to rest next to Mumtaz Mahal.

Aurangzeb expanded the Mughal empire geographically and lived in splendor for some time. He is known to have adorned himself with gold and jewels. Diamonds and topaz studded his clothing which was made of gold cloth and the finest silk. Pearls of unparalleled quality hung from his neck and draped over his stomach. His throne, constructed originally for Shah Jahan, contained a mass of diamonds and other jewels which were displayed to show the immense wealth accumulated by the dynasty. Aurangzeb's conquests, however, contributed to the eventual fall of the Mughal Empire, and Aurangzeb died a defeated man. His narrow religious outlook and intolerance to Hindus made him unpopular. Aurangzeb plunged into wasting wars in the Deccan, exhausting the treasury and extending the scope of the empire beyond what he could administrate.

The Mughal Empire (1526–1739) was the last of the great premodern Indian empires. It dominated the history of the subcontinent. Soon after Aurangzeb's death, the empire broke up. The nineteenth and the last Mughal ruler, Bahadur Shah II, was deposed by the British in 1858.

9

India's Landscape

"The roads to knowledge are many. One of the greatest for me began in a very unexpected way. We were coming up to the mouth of a jungle river and there were scattered islets in the approaches. On one of these I saw what appeared to be an interesting ruin and later, when I had some time, I hired a boy with a boat to sail me out there."

—Louis L'Amour,
from *Education of a Wandering Man*

Udhagamandalam is a world-class name by any standard, a tongue twister for most people not familiar with the place, a name that is intriguing enough to make it worth some effort to get there. Southern India is peppered with villages having musical names. Whenever a free day developed, we made the most of it by packing the car and heading out of Bangalore across the rural Indian countryside in search of one of these magical locations, knowing that something unusual was bound to happen.

Our search was as much for satisfaction as it was to find places that were off the beaten path. It was a means to quench our curiosity about the diverse nature of Indian life, about the geography in the region, and about the history that has made India what it is today. Passing from one area to the next was often more like changing countries than changing villages. In a day's drive there could be numerous transitions—where the languages of the local people differed, where the predominant religious and cultural makeups of the people were not the same, and where vast differences in geography led to vast differences in lifestyles. In one long day it was possible to travel from a city with a population of five million to rural desert communities, to jungles, to mountains, to tropical wetlands, and to coastal ocean communities.

Fortunately, Udhagamandalam had a second name that was easier to use in a conversation: Ooty (the anglicized name Ootacamund is shortened to Ooty). Several months after arriving in India, we took advantage of a two-day holiday by loading the Tata Estate with supplies and heading south into the Nilgiri mountains. Our destination was Ooty, an old British hill station, about eight hours drive from Bangalore. This was our first trip into the Indian heartland, our first chance to see the makeup of rural India.

For several hours, the highway made its way through rice-paddy farms, coconut plantations, and sugarcane estates. We passed through a number of small villages, over rivers, and along reservoirs. Villagers were threshing and separating grain on the rough pavement, expecting vehicles going by to drive through the pile of coarse material to help with the separation process. The landscape was peppered with unusual rock formations, some jutting vertically from the Deccan Plateau 500 meters or more.

As we followed the main highway south, we encountered the remains of many fresh vehicle collisions. Several were from the night before. The magnitude of the collisions seemed devastating. In one spot, a bus had collided head-on with a truck. In another, a Maruti van was flattened against a tree. Several kilometers further a sand truck had rolled over, ejecting the driver through the windshield. A bus lay on its side in a cane field. The remains of recent, but older, accidents had been shifted to the roadside, and burned-out hulls of public buses, old Ambassadors, and a variety of trucks appeared from time to time.

The terrain changed as our drive brought us into Bandipur Forest Reserve, a vast area with natural forest and jungle foliage. Bandipur is inhabited by wild tigers, elephants, leopards, deer, cobras, and other creatures indigenous to the subcontinent. The forest edge along the highway was routinely worked by tame elephants that pulled logs from the brush and helped to move other materials from place to place. These domestic beasts wandered loose along the roadside and could be identified by the rugged logging chain attached like a bracelet around one leg.

The road through the reserve was narrow, only wide enough for one vehicle at a time. Opposing cars found their own way around each other. Signs along the road identify "ACCIDENT ZONE – CLOSEST HOSPITAL 15K" with a hand-painted picture of a skull on the sign. The hospital, a two-room cement building with whitewashed walls and a cement floor was more of an outpost than a proper medical facility.

Midway through the reserve we stopped at the ranger's station, a small group of cement buildings with a canteen. Cathy and I got out of the car to look around while the children dug through our belongings to find the picnic food we had brought with us. A monkey dropped from the tree we were parked under and landed directly on the front hood of the car. The creature peered through the windshield. Another monkey jumped from the branch onto the luggage rack and looked over the side into the car. Suddenly several monkeys descended onto the Tata Estate, scratching at the windows from all sides and staring at the frightened children inside. Seeing the children as he emerged from one of the buildings, Selvan ran to the rescue, scattering the monkeys in all directions.

When we reached the far border of Bandipur, we passed through a crude road barrier into Mudumulai, another reserve, and were required to register with the forest service. The regristration form asked for *'vehicle identification number or description of animal.'* Much of the transportation in the country was done by animal. Mules and bulls pulling carts in this setting looked more in their element than those that mixed with Bangalore traffic during rush hour.

We left the state of Karnataka and entered Tamil Nadu, quickly commencing an uphill drive along the side of mountains in the Nilgiri range. The Nilgiris are rugged and covered with plush vegetation. Switchbacks on the narrow two-lane highway made the trip precarious. At every turn Selvan tapped the horn to communicate with unseen oncoming traffic. When we did encounter another car or truck, the smaller vehicle stopped to let the larger vehicle pass.

In places where the mountains had been tamed, rice paddies were cut into the steep slope, and small clusters of grass-roofed huts appeared from time to time. As the elevation increased, we emerged above the clouds into what could have been Shangri-La, where the rice terraces were replaced by tea plantations. Deep green tea bushes covered the mountainside like a thick quilt protecting the ground beneath. The mountain air smelled of tea, and streams of women walked single file down the mountain road with huge bundles of leaves balanced on their heads.

The road meandered through higher elevations into Ooty—nearly 2,300 meters. Ooty is a tourist spot, developed originally in the late 19th century for British expatriates. Families kept small cottages where a mother and children could stay for several months. Routinely, the father, with the typical British company or government annual leave, would come to the hill station for about six weeks. Eventually some sectors of the government relocated to Ooty so that the British families could spend more time together.

Only remnants of the British presence remained. Old cottages peppered the valley. A few old churches were on the side of the mountains, and there were several boarding schools still operating in the region. The original horse racetrack, though not well kept, still remained in the center of the valley, and a small mountain lake was situated on the outskirts of the city. The lake was almost entirely devoted to recreation, with a boat dock on one side where people could rent rowboats and paddle for a short distance.

On our first trip, we stayed in an old British estate that was akin to a bed and breakfast. Each room had a fireplace, and the walls were almost a meter thick. The ceiling was close to four meters high. Everything about the place maintained the aura of an old English manor. In the restaurant, a small green lizard crossed the floor as we finished our breakfast.

It was Sunday morning, and we drove further uphill to Doddabetta Peak, the highest ground in southern India. As with so many spots in India, cliffs were unprotected, allowing pedestrians to walk as close to the edge as their comfort would allow. From the peak we could see Ooty in the valley below. The mountain air was cool enough to make sweaters comfortable, and back at the hotel, a fire was burning in the fireplace at night.

The following day we drove to Coonor, another hill station, with more views of the mountains. Selvan knew of a dirt road leading to a remote lookout point called the Dolphin's Nose, overlooking a deep canyon with views of a tall waterfall on the opposite side of the valley. For those who could take their eyes off the road, the view was particularly spectacular on the route to the Dolphin's Nose. The road, which was not much more than a mud trail, made one switchback after another along the face of the mountain. On one side of the trail, the mountain dropped off into a sheer cliff. On the other side, it rose like a vertical wall.

Since this was a holiday weekend, there were several other vehicles following the same route to and from the Dolphin's Nose. Two were tourist buses. The road was so narrow that when a vehicle encountered opposing traffic, one needed to reverse to a spot where the other could get by. There were no guard rails. It was frightening to watch a bus squeeze by an oncoming Ambassador that had moved into a depression against the cliff wall. There were occasionally waterfalls sprinkling down from the mountain and crossing the road, making for muddy, washed-out areas where we watched passengers pile out of a car to push their vehicle forward a few meters until it reached a better spot in the road. We saw a Maruti van bottom out three times while trying to get by an oncoming truck. At one point the Maruti was suspended on its undercarriage, with no contact between the road and the rear wheels. The passengers pushed the van forward, with loud scraping sounds, and off the car went to its next obstacle.

Then there was the fight. Two vehicles came nose to nose, and both refused to give way. When we arrived, two cars were ahead of us, and vehicles were accumulating steadily in the other direction. Several dozen passengers from various vehicles were standing around as the two drivers hurled insults at each other. Some of the passengers were trying to restrain the drivers. Others looked like they wanted to get into the fight themselves. We stood back and waited curiously for the dust to settle. Finally, one driver picked up a large rock and threatened to throw it through the windshield of the other vehicle. Nearly forty-five minutes passed before the two managed to work out their differences and the crowd of spectators climbed back into their cars. By then, so many cars were backed up on this little road that recovering from the gridlock seemed impossible. One by one, however, the vehicles inched backward and forward, leapfrogging each other, until everyone was moving again.

One of the world's few remaining narrow-gauge train tracks connected Ooty with Coonor. The train had been in service since 1897. Its engine still pumped black smoke into the air as it traveled along the edge of the mountains, through tunnels cut in the rock, and over rickety bridges made of wood. The ride was simple, but the experience was nostalgic.

During our India assignment we made eight trips to Ooty. We eventually shifted from the bed and breakfast to a larger and more continental Holiday Inn. The Ooty Holiday Inn was a complete surprise to find in such an out-of-the-way place. The hotel was tucked into the steep side of the mountain and had many of the modern conveniences of luxury hotels anywhere in the world.

The Holiday Inn had an interesting coffee shop. We sat down for breakfast and were astonished to find a menu that read like it had come directly from Michigan: omelets, French toast with ham, and hotcakes with real maple syrup! Reading the menu made us drool. The children each ordered the hotcakes. Cathy went for an omelet.

"I would like the French toast with ham, please," I requested.

"Oh, sir," the waiter replied, "we have no ham today. Could you make another selection?"

"Hmm—no ham...Well, could you please bring just the French toast...and would you be willing to bring me some of the maple syrup that comes with the hotcakes."

"I'm sorry, sir, we do not have maple syrup." The children's expressions suddenly turned to looks of despair. "But I will bring you honey, sir." The children reached for the menus for another look. The corn flakes were looking quite good.

At dinner time the following day, we returned to the coffee shop. The dinner menu had a moderate but enticing selection of continental foods. The children all ordered southern fried chicken. I wondered what this would be like.

"I would like the pork chops," I told the dinner waiter when it became my turn.

"Sir, may I suggest the chicken. It is quite good."

I reviewed the menu one more time. "No, I think I'll stay with the pork chops."

"I'm sorry sir, we do not have pork chops today. I think you may like the chicken."

"Let me look at the menu for a few more minutes. Can you come back to finish the order?"

"A pleasure, sir." I reread the menu from top to bottom.

The waiter returned. "Could you please bring me the spaghetti?"

"Sir, you should try the chicken. It is an exceptional selection."

"No, I think I'll go with the spaghetti tonight."

"I'm sorry sir, we have no spaghetti today."

Hmm...no spaghetti, no pork chops—interesting," That's a shame. What do you have besides the chicken today?"

"No, sir, we only have the chicken today. I will bring it to you. It is an excellent selection."

"Thank you, I would really like the chicken tonight."

It was just before Christmas when we arrived for one visit. We sat in the room, viewing the panorama from our window and watching clouds roll in to engulf the valley below. Clouds in the Nilgiris looked like a thick bank of fog that formed a soft gray blanket—only the tips of the mountains protruded. When the clouds were in place, there was only an endless murky sea of gray with green-covered islands scattered across the surface. The sun was going down and lights were appearing one by one in the village in the valley below. I watched the darkness arrive before the cloud bank reached the village. There were tiny lights from the cottages peeping out in the darkness like stars below, and stars by the millions in the night sky above. It was as if we had found the center of the universe in this small mountain village in southern India.

We enjoyed visiting Ooty because of the spectacular drive to get there. Late in the afternoon on one of the trips, as we passed through Bandipur, we came upon three wild elephants in the forest near the roadside. Two adults and a small calf were using their long trunks to pull foliage from the lower branches of a tree and depositing the greens into their mouths. Selvan stopped our vehicle for a chance to photograph the animals. We slowly reversed to get a closer shot.

As luck would have it, a shiny white Ambassador rounded the bend from behind, motoring forward at normal speed for the road. The driver of the Ambassador caught a glimpse of the animals through his side window.

He pulled to a quick stop and put his vehicle in reverse to get a better view also. As his vehicle backed up, the music of "Jingle Bells" instantly began to play as a warning to anyone behind the vehicle. The largest of the elephants turned on its heels. Its trunk shot straight out and bellowed a threatening blast. The elephant charged through the brush, ignoring obstacles between it and the Ambassador. Selvan quickly put our vehicle into gear and started to move forward. The elephant skidded to a stop only two meters from the Ambassador, which was frozen in its tracks. With a quick spin, the elephant changed its target and charged after us. Selvan, with a look of fright on his face, moved as fast as he could.

"Slow down, Selvan. I want a picture of this!"

Selvan looked over his shoulder with a panicked expression on his face. "No Sir. Too dangerous."

The Tata Estate picked up speed. The elephant crashed through the brush parallel to the road, continuing to gain on us. Finally, we reached a speed that matched the elephant, and after another hundred meters the beast victoriously slowed to a jog and watched us disappear down the road.

During the last six months of our stay, a brigand named Veerappan and his band of followers who lived in the jungle of Bandipur and Mudumulai became a bit more aggressive than usual. Veerappan was one of India's most notorious outlaws from 1980 until 2000. He was a known elephant poacher, ivory seller, and sandalwood smuggler, responsible for the death of more than 150 Indian law officers and forest rangers. But he had a Robin Hood quality about him and was loved and protected by the local villagers in the rural area.

Veerappan had direct access to the press and was making overtures to gain amnesty during the time we were in India. He was reported to shift locations in the jungle on foot every night, frequently twenty kilometers or more. His band slept in the trees during the day and lived completely off the wild. Police made raid after raid, just missing him. They sent scouts and snipers into the jungle, but Veerappan continued to elude his pursuers.

To Veerappan, the ticket to amnesty was negotiation over hostages. He began stopping vehicles on the road through Bandipur, kidnapping passengers, and demanding top-level agreements for their release. Although he threatened to execute the hostages, they were always released in fine health after some time. Some of the hostages even reported that they had had the time of their lives, trekking through the bush at night, living off wild meat, sleeping in the jungle during the day, and eventually being returned to their families. Veerappan's antics cut Ooty's supply of tourists to a small trickle.

Nearing the end of our stay, Veerappan's activities subsided a bit. The road through Bandipur was opened on a limited basis, and we made a final dash to Ooty to feel the cool mountain air and see the splendid mountains for a final time. When approaching the reserve, a simple sign read: "VEERAPPAN ACTIVE IN REGION. PROCEED AT YOUR OWN RISK."

Veerappan eventually captured Raj Kumar, the famous South Indian movie star, holding him for a considerable time before finally releasing him unharmed. In the spring of 2002, while I was at a business meeting in Bangalore, one of my colleagues told me that he had just heard breaking news that Veerappan had finally been captured. I quickly called Cathy in Michigan to let her know the story. Cathy was with a friend from India at the time and quickly passed on the news. Later in the day I was reminded that it was the first of April. I considered the novelty that not only had I been completely taken in by this April foolery, but that I had passed on the rumor halfway around the world. Veerappan was finally killed by police in 2004.

Nandi Hills was a station close to Bangalore—we could get to and return home within one day. It was a picturesque spot in the desert. The road to the top was steep, climbing to about 1,600 meters. It was not uncommon to pass three or four disabled vehicles on the way up, overheated from the climb.

This mountain was really one of several huge granite features rising off the desert floor. The area is of historical significance since it was the spot where Tipu Sultan lured the British army to strategically make battle conditions more favorable for himself. From the top, the mountain drops off as a sheer cliff on one side, known as the Tipu Drop. It is said that having lured the British to the peak, Tipu sent many of them back to the bottom over the edge of the cliff.

An ancient temple, still in service, was constructed on the bare rock surface close to the mountain peak, near the Tipu Drop. A second, much smaller temple was tucked into the side of a cliff near the top, using the natural surface as one of its walls. Families with picnic meals claimed their spots on the bare granite near the Tipu Drop to relax and enjoy the panoramic view that encircled them.

Mysore was three hours by car south of Bangalore. Known for its pleasant climate, it was originally the seat of the Maharajas of Mysore. It was the home of the large and ornate Ambavilas Palace, the ruins of Srirangapatna, one of Hyder Ali and Tipu Sultan's original forts, and Chamundi Hill, with its four-meter-tall stone statue of Nandi, Siva's bull. There was also an impressive temple of the goddess Chamundeshwari at the top of a hill close to the city. Mysore was the location of India's best zoo, with rhinos, giraffes, elephants, deer, leopards, and panthers. The habitat for the animals was left nearly in a wild state, and visitors were permitted quite close access to the creatures.

We stayed at the Southern Star Hotel whenever we were in Mysore. Mysore is by nature a tourist town, and a good side attraction for travelers who have made it as far as Bangalore. This meant that most spots where tourists might be, were also populated by a large contingent of touts. With a smile on their faces, they played and marketed their musical instruments made from coconut shells or bamboo. They had boxes of old coins for sale. One man in a turban sat cross-legged outside of our hotel lobby with a small cigar box and a flute. He tapped on the box as we went out to call for our car. The man played a mysterious tune on his flute and opened the box, hoping that the cobra inside would raise up and show its face. The snake lay sleeping in the bottom of the box.

"Sir," the charmer called to us. He closed the box and tapped on the lid with his flute. "Please, for my cobra." He pushed forward a small tin dish with some coins in it and began to play his flute again. The cobra continued to sleep. We walked by.

"Please, sir." He knocked on the side of the box trying to stir the cobra. We got in the car. The man poked in the box cautiously, hoping not to get bitten. The snake continued to sleep. "Please, sir. For my cobra."

Nick stepped out of the car and put five rupees into the tin dish. With a wide toothless grin, the charmer put the flute to his mouth and began to play a melody. The snake continued its nap. A small green lizard peered out from behind the curb where the charmer was sitting.

Driving from Mysore, the remote and beautiful Shimsha falls were reachable in just a few hours. The falls were tall, powerful, and completely accessible. During the monsoon season, rain ensures plenty of water gushing over the cliff.

Many places like this in India were undeveloped and had little or no commercialization. A grass clearing at the end of the dirt road served as a parking spot for people viewing the falls. A small, deserted concrete cabana had been constructed for a lookout at one of the best viewing locations. Near the edge of the clearing, a man with a small pile of coconuts and a machete was selling tender coconut water to the few people who ventured his way.

We walked to the riverbank at the top of the falls. A man sat on a rock in the river while water gushed around him over the cliff to a pool more than fifty meters below. Angie, Nick, and I disappeared down a small foot trail that led to the bottom of the gorge, where the water misted up into the air, mixing with the rays of sunlight to form a small rainbow.

Halebid—The Nandi Bull (1996)

Goa—Ruins of the Portuguese Fort (1998)

Along a Rural Road (1997)

**Road Repair Team Along a National Highway
in Rural India (1997)**

**A Device Constructed to Pull a
Tanker Back Up to the Road (1997)**

The Tanker That Had Gone Over the Cliff (1997)

Hampi (1998)

Hampi (1998)

Selvan at Coonor Train Station (1997)

Renukoot City Street (1998)

Commercial Street—Bangalore (1996)

Bangalore City Street (1997)

Elevated Rail Public Transit – Bengaluru (2022)

Bengaluru (2022)

10

The British Raj

"As long as we rule India, we are the greatest power in the world. If we lose it, we shall drop straight-away to a third-rate power."

—Lord Curzon, British Viceroy of India,1898–1905

When the East India Company was first granted a charter in 1600 by Queen Elizabeth I, its commercial focus was not on the Indian subcontinent. Although the English knew of India, and a sea route had been successfully navigated by the Portuguese explorer Vasco da Gama in 1498, India was considered a less attractive area with which to develop trade than spice islands such as Java, Sumatra, and the Celebes. Some of these Indonesian kingdoms already maintained strong trade relationships with Dutch and Portuguese merchants. The original East India Company began with more than 200 investors. Their products, spices used to preserve meat throughout the European winters, were expected to be in great demand in England.

The first voyage set out on October 8, 1600, with five ships carrying a total of 500 men and with a combined capacity of 1,500 tons. Queen Elizabeth commissioned the company to mint coinage specifically for trade in Asia and forbade the use of other foreign coins in their commerce. All silver exported was to have the Queen's effigies and picture coined on one side and a portcullis on the other. "Her prudent reason for this was that her name and the effigies might hereafter be respected by the Asiatic, and she be known as great a prince as the King of Spain" (Thurston, p. 7). The coins were known as India money.

The East India Company enjoyed nearly a quarter of a century of successful trading in the Indonesian region, coexisting to some degree with the Dutch, until 1623 when all-out military and political competition between the two made it much more risky for the English to continue there. Meanwhile, in 1608 an English ship had rounded the Cape of Good Hope at the southern tip of Africa and sailed in a more northerly direction to Surat, a Portuguese port on the west coast of India. From there William Hawkins, a representative of the East India Company, traveled over land to Agra to petition Jahangir, the Mughal emperor, for English trading rights in the region. Hawkins' request was granted on a limited basis in 1612, only after Jahangir knew of an English defeat of the Portuguese in a sea battle near Surat. Several years later Sir Thomas Roe, after spending more than three years as an ambassador in the emperor's court, was able to convince Jahangir to allow expansion of the English presence on the subcontinent, permitting trade centers to be developed at a number of ports along the coast. The English maintained Surat as their primary base.

By 1690, the East India Company had established Fort St. George in Madras (Chennai today), Fort St. William in Calcutta (Kolkata today), and also a fort in Bombay (Mumbai today). Bombay was in fact given to King Charles II in 1661 as a part of the dowry from his Portuguese bride, Princess Catherine of Braganza. King Charles rented the entire city to the East India Company for trading interests of the English.

It did not take long for the East India Company to realize that their resources in India presented

112

opportunities that went beyond the trading of raw goods. Manufactured items could be even more lucrative since the value of labor to convert raw silk into silk cloth, or raw cotton into a finished product, was in England "a great deal dearer than the labour by which the same could be wrought in India" (Judd, 1972, p. 22). The cost of transporting finished textile goods to England was the same as transporting the same weight in raw materials.

During the 17th century, the East India Company faced many commercial and political challenges. In addition to developing a new company and operating in regions that were entirely unfamiliar to the English, there were power struggles within India itself: challenges to the Mughal Empire and positioning between the Muslim and Hindu kingdoms. Periodic famines swept the subcontinent, weakening the company's financial position. The Dutch and the Portuguese, aggressive commercial competitors, also proved to be strong military adversaries on land and at sea.

To make matters worse, competition from within England started in 1698 when King William permitted the formation of the New East India Company, a second English company free to trade in the region. Internal competition weakened both companies sufficiently that, within ten years, the two companies merged as a matter of survival. In 1708, the United Company of Merchants of England Trading to the East Indies was formed with a charter from the British government guaranteeing the company a monopoly for British trade in India. This British East India Company became the dominant military and commercial power in India for nearly 150 years. The company fought the Dutch, Portuguese, French, and local Mughal princes to seize control over the region piece by piece and defend its commercial interests.

In 1756, Siraj-ud-duala, the Nawab of Bengal, in alliance with the French, attacked the British East India Company's fort in Calcutta, imprisoning 146 Europeans in a small dark room, later known as the Black Hole of Calcutta. During the night, 123 of the prisoners died. A year later, Robert Clive, the East India Company governor of Fort St. David, joining forces with Mir Jafar, a local noble, defeated Siraj-ud-duala's army of 50,000 men, with the help of only 900 British soldiers and 2,300 Indian troops. Mir Jafar was installed as the new Nawab of Bengal, and the East India Company "by paying a yearly rental of 27,000 pounds to Mir Jafar, was recognized as supreme landlord of 882 square miles around Calcutta. In 1759, in return for aid in suppressing a rebellion, Mir Jafar agreed to remit to Clive annually the rental paid by the company" (Durant, 1967, p. 715).

Similar alliances across the subcontinent with the East India Company supporting, if not reconstructing, local political regimes in a way that they would be favorable to British trade were the hallmark of the East India Company. The company maintained a strong military presence. British protection of local rulers was accompanied by considerable coercion and was rarely considered voluntary by the local ruler.

Back in England, the view of tactics being used to manage India drew strong criticism from directors of the Company as well as the public. Reports of widespread corruption and unnecessary brutality surfaced. Several parliamentary investigations were initiated to determine whether British administrators were going beyond what was proper. "We have murdered, deposed, plundered, usurped," Horace Walpole orated in 1772 (Durant, 1967, p. 716). Robert Clive and, later, Warren Hastings were both called back to England to defend their brutal practices. Both were accused of corruption and reaping excessive personal gain from their powerful positions. Both defended their actions by contending that what they had done fit well within the local context and customs, and that the end justified the means. In fact, financial returns of the East India Company were more than satisfying to the shareholders during this period, and both the East India Company and England turned a blind eye to what was being done to sustain England's successful trading advantage.

During this period, a social structure slowly evolved in India that put the British in a class of their own. As a relatively small group of foreigners, British were well educated, wealthier than all but Indian royalty, and wielded a large amount of commercial power. The British position was backed by a military with superior discipline and weaponry. From the beginning, the British had an attitude of superiority. Over more than a century of supporting only local leaders sympathetic to British ways, replacing those who were not, and developing an Indian dependence on British commerce, an attitude of inferiority to the British seemed to evolve in the common Indian. Foreigners took on a position equal to, but separate from Indian royalty. As more British citizens came to India and the feasibility of bringing a family from Europe increased, a separate British society began to develop within India.

As was the case with Indian royalty, so, too, the British few amassed wealth and enjoyed a high standard of living at the expense of the Indian people in the lower castes. An endless supply of servant laborers allowed the British a means to build surroundings that in some ways duplicated those of upper-class England. While at the time the extensive use of servant labor was probably not considered exploitative in an Indian context, the heavy-handed dominance by the British over local Indian rulers evolved into what was considered by the Indians an oppressive manipulation of Indian society, culture, and resources.

The British, at least in some circles, had a different view of the situation. Some developed an attitude of responsibility for the Indian people, who they viewed as subjects under their stewardship. To facilitate this the British began to educate a fairly elite group of Indians in the English language through the British educational system. Thomas Macaulay argued in 1835, "We must at present do our best to form a class who may be interpreters between us and the millions we govern; a class of persons, Indian in blood and colour, but English in taste, in opinions, in morals, and in intellect" (Judd, 1972, p. 55). A thread of social improvements implemented by the British began to appear in the early 19th century including establishing educational institutions available to some Indians, agricultural technology advancements, and plans to establish a rail system on the subcontinent. Some would say that these changes were self-serving for the British.

Administrators of the East India Company began to institute laws in the subcontinent that they viewed as humanitarian efforts. For instance, it was not uncommon in north India for a Hindu widow to throw herself on the burning funeral pyre of her dead husband, a practice called *sati,* often encouraged by Indian families but declared illegal by British administration in 1829. Unwanted female babies were often killed at birth because they would result in a burden for the family, both in care and in dowries that would be expected at the time of marriage. Again, administrators from the East India

Company attempted to reform the age-old practice. In the 1830s the company also tried to root out a sect of thieves who would perform *thugee*, strangling their victims as a sacrifice to the goddess Kali. At the time, these *thugs* were considered some of the most cunning robbers in the world.

The army managed by the East India Company was made up of officers from the British military and a large concentration of local Indian troops paid by the East India Company. The military was funded by subsidies paid annually by the local rulers to the company. This structure had been in place and working successfully for many decades. British officers juggled the challenges of managing boredom and scandalous behavior within their own ranks and often used iron-handed, if not inhumane, disciplinary tactics on the Indian regiments.

In 1857 when a new version of the Enfield rifle was introduced, the loading procedure required a soldier to bite the end of the cartridge. This was a problem for the Muslim and Hindu troops. The Indians believed the cartridges had been coated with animal fat as a part of the manufacturing process. Muslims considered pigs to be unclean and refused to load the cartridges. Hindus believed that cattle were sacred and refused to load the cartridges. As a matter of discipline, the British commander publicly reprimanded 85 Indian cavalry soldiers, stripping them of the medals they had earned in service and sentencing them to ten years in prison.

The following day, Indian regiments in Bengal rose up in mutiny, slaughtering their British officers. This incident sparked a rebellion that immediately spread across northern India, supported by a large number of civilians opposing British dominance and releasing years of pent-up feelings of oppression. But the rebellion was disorganized. It had inadequate central leadership and no unified objective. In just over one year, and with an uncompromising exertion of ruthless force, British troops crushed their opposition and ended the Sepoy Mutiny. Three months later the British government announced the takeover of the administration of the territories in India from the British East India Company, appointing a Viceroy in India and a Secretary of State for India in London. The army in India was also reformed to limit the ratio of Indian troops to British troops to not exceed two Indian soldiers for one British soldier.

So began, in 1858, the slow process by Britain of establishing a system of government, the British Raj, to span the Indian subcontinent. It included a viceroy, who by 1900 was responsible for more than 300 million subjects. Below the viceroy, regional governors were installed to oversee provinces. Although she never visited India, Queen Victoria was proclaimed Empress of India in 1877.

It was the responsibility of the British Raj to enforce law and maintain order, to improve the infrastructure of the country, and to sort out social problems such as health and education. For Britain, the importance of India went beyond altruism. India accounted for a major portion of British foreign investment. By 1900, India was the destination of 19 percent of all exports leaving England. The British government introduced irrigation projects, built rail systems, encouraged industrial development, provided relief for famine, established educational institutions, and built hospitals. Their efforts, however, continued in a patronizing spirit. "The British in India tended to stress that they had a noble mission in ruling a lesser people for their own good" (Judd, 1972, p. 85).

When India entered the twentieth century, a legitimate movement for independence from Britain had not yet begun. The seeds, however, had been planted through many decades of British dominance over the Indian people. As the small group of Indians educated within the British system began to grow, the need for political reform in both practice and policy became necessary. For instance, what good was it to educate an Indian as a barrister in the British/Indian legal system if the individual was not permitted to practice law? The political changes, though obviously required in retrospect, did not come easily at the time and frequently led to an amplification of deep-seated fear and prejudice by the British living in India. In turn, they produced a resentment of British oppressors by educated Indians.

Some British could see that time would eventually lead India to self-governance but could identify no practical or humane way of avoiding what eventually must happen. They could, however, slow down or delay the inevitable. Bit by bit British government supported small reform, primarily to appease the Indian people and avoid all-out rebellion, but also as improvements for the Indian people. In 1885, the Indian National Congress was permitted to be formed as a forum for discussion among educated Indians, a forum strongly supported by the British. In 1909, one Indian was admitted to the Viceroy's Executive Council, and Indians were given more strength in local legislative councils. By 1919, the Viceroy's Executive Council was modified to include three Indians and four British.

Still, all was not well. In the same year, during an Indian demonstration in Amritsar, a British general in the sector ordered troops to open fire on the crowd. More than 400 Indian demonstrators were killed. The wounded count exceeded one thousand. Public outcry was enormous, and the event sparked an organized independence movement. Yet it would take more than a quarter of a century for the movement to come to fruition—twenty-five more years of colonialism, prejudice, and festering resentment.

11

Ancient Sites

"The road proceeds from Moorshedabad through the villages of Jungepoor and Sooty to Oodooanullah. This road is crossed by several nullahs, some of which have ferry boats stationed at them to accommodate the traveler. At the last-mentioned place is a bridge, built by Sultan Sujah, the second son of the Emperor Shah Jehan, who was appointed Subah of the province of Bengal, one hundred and thirty years ago. This is one of the most elegant specimens in architecture of those times; and it has become famous in ours by the victory obtained over troops of Meer Cossim, in the year 1764, by the late Major Adams."

—William Hodges, 1793,
from *Travels in India During the Years 1780, 1781, 1782, 1783*

India's countryside is filled with antiquity. Century-old shrines, often passed over because they are nothing unusual, can be found throughout the rural countryside. They are often overgrown with vegetation, tree roots breaking through their foundations, and missing stones used a second time to construct a more recent structures close by. Frequently while traveling along the back roads, one sees the crumbling remains of an old fortress wall, crowning the peak of a rugged hill. These ancient sites, interesting by most standards, are nearly overshadowed by the historic places that India is known for.

Three twelfth-century temples were within driving reach of Mysore. The layout of each temple was unique, but the intricate friezes on the exterior of each clearly made them cousins of each other. The temple at Somnathpur, the smallest and least visited, was located in cane fields, on the edge of a small rural village far off the beaten path. Every stone making up the temple was carved with battle scenes featuring warriors on elephant back, horseback, or foot.

Channakeshava Temple at Belur was still a working Hindu temple. Geometric pillars surrounded the interior of the main wall. A temple chariot was visible in one bay near the entrance. The large courtyard had been reconstructed from stones at the site, forming a patio with a patchwork appearance. With the Indian sun glaring onto the stone surface, we tiptoed in shoeless feet from block to block, finding ancient inscriptions or carvings on the walking surface. The temple's open courtyard provided few shadows to walk in. In our bare feet, we felt like we were crossing a hot frying pan to reach the gate where we could retrieve our footwear.

Unlike Channakeshava Temple, Hoysaleswara Temple at Halebid was not enclosed by a surrounding wall. This temple was considered to be the most outstanding example of temple artwork during the 12th century. Its surfaces were covered from head to toe with detailed depictions of animal caravans, battle scenes, deities, and dancing maidens. The stone roofs to one side of the temple sheltered two massive stone sculptures of Nandi, the bull.

The temple grounds were manicured gardens, with mowed grass stretching over much of the property. To the rear of the temple, individual carved stones had been arranged in an organized fashion in an unkempt field, providing the atmosphere of an active archaeological site. This area, though officially off limits to the public, was not monitored. A walk through the old stones was like looking over the pieces of a larger-than-life jigsaw puzzle that would reveal an ancient secret once it was reassembled. At the entrance to the Hoysaleswara Temple grounds, a small museum had been erected to display examples of the twelfth-century temple carvings. A large and impressive monolithic Jain statue was placed in a prominent spot in the temple garden. Signs forbidding photography of the monolith gave it an immediate aura of importance, which was reinforced by the gardeners who kept a close eye on any cameras in the area and immediately approached tourists who looked like they might attempt to sneak a shot of the huge nude male.

Local tradition suggests that a Hindu should first visit Halebid and then proceed to Belur. Halebid means "an abode which has fallen to ruins." The local belief is that if a visitor to Halebid goes home or elsewhere directly from Halebid, ill luck is sure to follow. To avoid this fate, a visitor must visit Halebid, then the Belur Temple, and then return home.

We were impressed by the Jain statue at Halebid until we arrived at Sravana Belagola. Selvan parked the car at the foot of a 300-meter rock hill protruding straight up from the desert surface and directed us down a narrow alley of dusty craft vendors to the booth where we could leave our shoes. Wandering down the walkway in bare feet, we knew we were already on sacred ground. The long path to the top of the steep cliff was made of steps individually carved into the single granite rock more than 1,000 years ago. Several men waited at the bottom with a bamboo chair supported by two long poles to transport pilgrims not fit for the climb. We arrived late in the morning, hoping to avoid the most severe heat on the rock while we walked more than 1,000 steps to the top.

John, our guest on one trip, was more than eighty years old. At the temple entrance we paid a fee and arranged porters with a bamboo chair to transport John to the top. Signs instructed us not to tip the porters since their wages were organized by the temple. Though the signs were not unusual, the policy seemed a bit strange in India, the land where tips were so common.

As John's porters began a quick jog to the top, we started a methodical single-file walk. Three rest areas had been recently carved into the granite at intervals along the way, and a galvanized pipe handrail mounted along the center of the staircase separated those going up from those coming down. As we approached the last rest area, I noticed John talking with the porters. I stepped into the conversation. One of the porters smiled somewhat shyly, showing the teeth missing from his mouth, and held out his hand.

"Sir," he said quietly, asking for a tip.

I was quite irritated. Here we were, thirty meters from the temple wall and the porters wanted money. John did not know what to do.

"You know, the signs at the bottom say no tips." I replied.

"Yes, sir. But no."

"I will give you a tip anyway, but not until we reach the bottom safely."

"Sir." The porters each picked up one end of the pole and delivered John to the ancient wall at the top of the rock.

As we walked through the wall, the centuries peeled away, with the primitive stone preserving years of religious antiquity. Simple block stairs inside the first wall led to a second passageway, and then a third. We emerged into an open area at the crown of the rock and could see the desert stretching out before us with a view of another temple on a lower hill on the far side of the village. The Jain temple we had climbed to see was only a few meters across the granite rock. Ancient Buddhist, Jain, and Hindu inscriptions were carved into the rock surface. As we walked through the inner temple entrance and into the final courtyard, we could see the feet of what was the largest and most amazing statue we had seen. This ancient nude male, reported to be the world's tallest monolithic statue, stood seventeen meters from the ground. A full-grown human was no taller than its ankle. How had it come to be built in this spot? How could it have been done in 980 CE, at the top of a steep rock 300 meters above the village on the desert floor? This spot immediately went to the top of my list.

We walked out of the temple wall, back into modern India, with the porters waiting to deliver John to the bottom. The sun had turned the granite into a skillet. Descending the staircase was nearly as taxing as the journey up had been. John's porters began a furious run down, with John bouncing in fright as they made each step. Halfway to the bottom, we again overtook the porters, who had stopped and were arguing with an exasperated John.

"Sir?" The leader said as he held out his hand.

"I will pay a tip," I replied angrily, "but not until we reach the bottom safely."

"But sir..."

"Not before we reach the bottom. And I want you to take it a bit slower for the rest of the way down, or there will be no tip."

The porters picked up their pole and gently walked to the bottom with John.

As I reached the last step, I pulled a 100 rupee note from my pocket and discreetly handed it to the lead porter. He placed his hands together, touching his forehead with the tip, and, with a bow, watched as we walked back to the shoe rack. A small green lizard darted off one of the shelves as the attendant handed us our shoes.

India's east coast, the Coromandel coast, bordering the Bay of Bengal, contains several historic or resort destinations. To visit one, we traveled east from Bangalore to Chennai, formerly known as Madras, and then south along the shore to an ancient village called Mahabalipuram. This site was known for its 700 CE stone temples and rock carvings. The temples were close to the beach and had been weathered by the salt water and heavy ocean winds. A number of the temples had been sculpted from a single rock rather than being built by the traditional method of adding one stone to another. The interior of the single stone was removed, leaving handsomely carved pillars to support the integrated roof.

While we stood in the parking area, trying to determine the best route through the ancient structures and outdoor markets that seemed to be in every direction, I felt the familiar presence of Kirk standing on my foot and tugging at my pants pocket. Looking out over the seashore and the landscape, I reached down to give Kirk a gentle pat on the head. I was shocked to find a small monkey, dressed in an ornately decorated red jacket and trousers, hanging on to my leg. A thin man asking for a few coins held one end of the leash. A green lizard scampered up the scrappy trunk of the windswept tree that provided a little shade for the monkey and its master.

Stone carving in Mahabalipuram had been passed down from generation to generation since the time the temples were built. Along the streets many people were at work carving in stone. Mahabalipuram was famous throughout India for the temples and the stone carving.

Only twenty kilometers from Mahabalipuram was a sea resort known as Fisherman's Cove. Fisherman's cove was constructed on the foundation of an old Dutch fort built in the 14th century. Remains of the old fort wall were still visible. The beach, though quite narrow near the resort, was nice, with moderate waves and few people. We walked the beach during the early morning and came to the spot where fishermen were launching their crude boats into the ocean. These hand-hewn crafts were constructed from five coconut trunks made square and tied together with ropes. A rough mast extended vertically from the center of each vessel, with a ragged sail attached to the mast. Large flat boards were used as paddles. Boats sailed beyond the horizon to cast their nets. Hundreds of these boats provided the subsistence living for families on the beach. During the monsoon season, storms often swept dozens of fishermen out to sea, where they were presumed lost in the depths of the ocean. We imagined these fishermen paddling their raft-like boats with board-like paddles toward the dark clouds on the horizon, hoping to return to the beach with a respectable catch before the weather grew worse.

The most extensive archaeological site we visited in southern India was Hampi, the legendary capital of the Vijayanagara Empire. This impressive spot was infrequently visited because it was so difficult to get to. It was about one long day's drive north of Bangalore in rugged desert territory, an area geographically unique because of the massive boulders laying like grains of sand on a beach, covering a 350-square-kilometer area, with the Tungabhadra River snaking down the center of the region. The road was often problematic, with frequent potholes, washouts, and trail-like conditions.

Domingo Paes, a Portuguese visitor, wrote about Hampi in 1520: "What I saw seemed as large as Rome, and very beautiful to the sight...the best provided city in the world" (Srinivasachar, p. 17).

Hampi was so extensive that it would take much more than a week to tour the area properly. We had two days. The ruins included structures scattered across the area, hidden behind boulders, concentrated in small villages, constructed on prominent hilltops, or laid out in narrow valleys. Some form of excavation was in progress at many of the ruins, but access to every area was without restriction.

One of the most impressive structures was the Vittala temple, constructed with ornately-carved monolithic columns and a stone chariot carved from a single rock. The stone columns were known to have a musical quality, each tuned to resonate at a specific note when tapped. The eerie music produced by the stone columns accented the desolate atmosphere of these empty buildings that had once been occupied by a vibrant community.

As we traveled by car from one site to another and walked from one shrine to the next, we passed intricate rock carvings of Hindu deities, battle scenes, and long processions of elephants. A trail led up one hillside, through a cave made from massive boulders leaning against each other, to a small shrine hidden in this labyrinth of stones.

We marveled at the geometry of the perfectly preserved stepped tank near the royal enclosure. Not far away, a mysterious underground passageway led us into complete darkness as it made several turns underground. Without a torch, we cautiously advanced to the second entrance by feeling the walls along the way.

We walked through the ruins of one abandoned bazaar after another, with columns lining the sidelines and lintels spanning from one column to the next, only imagining these streets filled with vendors and travelers, camels loaded with cargo and royal elephants escorting foreign traders through the marketplace. A small green lizard sunned itself in an empty street, while six men worked to replace a lintel that had rested on the ground nearby its supporting columns for nearly five centuries.

Travelers wishing to visit the India's most famous historic monument, the Taj Mahal, could do so quite easily by arranging an excursion out of Delhi. Our guests had planned such a trip, hoping to travel with us by rail to Agra to see this distinguished site. We had confirmed seats on the train from Delhi to Agra but had not been in the train station in Delhi before. I looked at our tickets as we entered the station. A well-dressed man with a friendly smile approached me.

"Can I help you, sir?" he asked politely while looking over my shoulder at the ticket confirmation.

"I'm looking for the platform that our train leaves from."

"Let me take a look." He picked up the confirmation sheet. "Oh sir, there may be a problem. This is a reservation sheet, not a confirmation. To find out what your seat is, you must look at the passenger list posting on the window of the office on the first floor." He raised his arm pointing to a dark staircase. "If you need help, there will be a man at the top of the stairs who can assist you."

Suppressing an irreverent thought about the travel agent who had arranged the ticket, I shepherded our guests to the staircase. We stepped over one person after another sleeping on the steps with gray blankets pulled over their heads. The first floor was empty, and the office doors were locked. A guard stood huddled against the wall with a blanket pulled over his shoulders.

"Excuse me, I was told that there is a posting of train passengers on this floor. Can you show me where it is?"

"Let me see, sir." The guard looked at our paper. "There is a man who will help you." He handed the papers back and walked around a corner, returning almost immediately with a young man in a business suit.

"May I see your information please?" We handed him the paperwork. "Sir, there is a problem. This is a reservation, not a confirmed seat. I can help you fix this. Come with me." We followed the young professional down the stairs to the ground floor, stepping over the people sleeping as we went.

"Where do we need to go to sort this out?"

"You see sir, the main offices are closed now. I do know a travel agent across the street who can help you at this hour."

My radar activated as we followed him. He was leading us away from the main railway entrance to a back door that led into an isolated alley.

"This is not right." I stopped. "Why do we need to leave the train station?"

"No, sir." He pointed to the darkness outside. "The office is only out here a short distance."

"Something is wrong here!" We turned and walked toward the main entrance of the station. I glanced over my shoulder. The young man in the suit had disappeared.

We walked to the train station information desk. "Could you please look at this paperwork and tell me if everything is in order."

"Yes, sir," the attendant inspected the sheet. "Your platform will be the one through the opening to the left. You have confirmed seats on the third car. Departure will be in twenty minutes."

"You know, there was this man—" I started to explain but stopped short. "Never mind. It doesn't matter." We set off to enjoy our journey to Agra.

The Taj Mahal is renowned for its tranquility, beauty, symmetry, craftsmanship, and the love story that led to its construction. The road from Delhi to Agra was the one most traveled by tourists visiting the subcontinent. It was a modern highway, more organized than most in India, with the rail line running on a parallel path to the road. Tourists, whether traveling by rail or by car, were bound to see camels pulling wagons loaded high with agricultural products as they traveled by car or train. Ancient Mughal military supply towers were also visible at regular intervals along the road.

The town of Agra was India's most aggressive tourist experience and also perhaps the place in India that was the least representative of the country's culture. Every tourist was a target for waves of local entrepreneurs. Money flowed like water. It seemed that every resident was a hustler of sorts. It was nearly impossible to navigate the city without surrendering to this unified brigade of sharks. In fact, the only peace to be had in Agra was within the walls of the Taj Mahal itself. The majesty of this site, however, was worth the battle fought in the streets to get to it.

The Agra Red Fort is located on the banks of the Yamuna River, within sight of the Taj Mahal. Shah Jahan, the ruler who built the Taj Mahal as a mausoleum for his wife, lived in the Red Fort while the Taj Mahal was being constructed. As the story goes, he was eventually held prisoner in the fort by his son in order to prevent him from building a duplicate mausoleum in black for himself on the opposite side of the river, a project that would have depleted the finances of the kingdom.

The Agra Red Fort was surrounded by two walls and a moat. In its day, the moat was inhabited by crocodiles. The area between the walls was a jungle with lions and tigers, making the fort nearly impenetrable.

Another ancient treasure in the Agra region was Fatehpur Sikri, located about one hour's drive west of the city, near the Rajasthan border. This impressive area developed by Akbar in the mid-1500s was less visited than the Taj Mahal and included well-preserved palaces, mosques, and fortresses, with a conscious integration of Persian and Hindu architecture. This site was one of the best-preserved antiquities in India, so well preserved that today it is like a ghost town.

Jama Masjid, the mosque at Fatehpur Sikri, was one of the most impressive structures of the site. Its tall gate at the entrance, Buland Darwaza, is said to be a copy of the mosque at Mecca. As we left our shoes on the steps by the main gate and reverently passed through the Arabian style arch, we felt like we were stepping into a different age and a different culture. We crossed the courtyard on the ancient paving stones and looked up to see a green lizard scamper across the mosque wall.

12

Independence

"A moment comes, which comes but rarely in history, when we step out of the old to the new, when an age ends, and when the soul of a nation long suppressed, finds utterance."

—Jawaharlal Nehru, August 14, 1947, addressing the Constituent Assembly in Delhi

One morning, Kirk slipped his backpack over his shoulders and, holding my hand, walked down the granite stairs outside the entrance to our flat. We were on our way to the car park area in the basement so that Selvan could drive him to school for another day of second grade.

"Who do you think gave us independence?" Kirk asked me.

I was shocked. I had never thought of the question in those terms before. The United States was more than 200 years old. Britain is perhaps now one of the strongest allies of the United States. It was hard to think of being a British colony. How do you answer such a question? I began to think—well, you know, Kirk. Hmm— there was the Revolutionary War and...

"Was it Gandhi or was it the British?" Kirk's question continued before I could finish my original thought.

I was surprised again. Kirk was thinking of himself as a citizen of India rather than as an American expatriate. The question made me connect with something I had known from a distance but had not ever considered relevant to my own life—the fact that the United States had also become independent from Britain. Before Kirk asked the question related to India, this fact about the United States seemed so far in the past. Now I wondered what it must be like for people living today in India, with the event happening during their own lifetimes. In the United States individuals today know that historically they have become independent from Britain. Individuals living in India today have *experienced* that they have become independent from Britain.

When Mohandas Karamchand Gandhi stepped off a boat from South Africa in 1915, he already had a notion of how civil protest could be conducted in calculated, nonviolent ways to bring about change on a large scale. Born in India and educated as a barrister, Gandhi moved to South Africa at the age of twenty-four to establish his career. Before long, Gandhi joined the movement of resistance to rampant racism in South Africa. He discovered that by peacefully and intentionally disobeying laws, encouraging participation in mass arrests, and promoting protest rallies, the masses could influence the underlying infrastructure and politics of a country.

Gandhi, a pious Hindu, had a vision of India that would unite its inhabitants and reestablish the dominance of traditional Indian civilization. Gandhi believed that the basic ideals of common Indian people were superior to the ideals imported by the Portuguese, Dutch, and the British. "Truth lay in morality, in one's own conscience and the performance of one's duty" (Memon & Banerji, p. 20). Gandhi's challenge was to unite the widely diverse peasant masses who differed in religion, language, and customs to peaceful protest in a way that would give the region its autonomy and thereby preserve the traditional Indian way of life.

In the end, Gandhi achieved only a portion of what he intended. While the region gained its independence, perhaps peacefully, from the British, its unification as envisioned by Gandhi was neither complete nor peaceful. The subcontinent was separated along religious lines, Hindu and Muslim, forming two independent countries, India and Pakistan. The geographical partition to facilitate religious differences resulted in mass relocation of the region's people, often accompanied by bloodshed and violence. Territorial disputes between India and Pakistan over the Jammu and Kashmir regions existed from the outset and have continued until today. And finally, Gandhi himself, the man of peace, was laid to rest by an assassin's bullet on January 30, 1948, only a few months after India gained her independence.

During the thirty-two years between Gandhi's arrival in India and Indian independence, Gandhi not only established friendships and alliances with members of the Indian leadership but also developed a following of the Indian common people. Gandhi was associated with three grassroots political-social movements, the Non-Co-operation Movement of 1920–1922, the Civil Disobedience Movement of 1930–1933, and the Quit India Movement of 1942. Gandhi became revered as a Mahatma, a great one.

When independence finally came in 1947, it came due to a confluence of historical factors and current events. The Second World War had drawn to a close, and Britain found herself needing to focus on rebuilding her own nation at home, with fewer resources to support activity in a troublesome colony plagued by cultural differences, complex internal alliances, and volatile political-social clashes. As Jawaharlal Nehru, the first Prime Minister of India, addressed a midnight session of the Constituent Assembly in Delhi on August 14, 1947, the umbrella of British rule over India closed. The morning of August 15, 1947 began afresh, with India in control of her own destiny.

Laying the groundwork for the hand-over was complex, a final task facilitated by the British Viceroy, Lord Mountbatten, and Sardar Vallabhbhai Patel, the first Home Minister of Independent India, a task that must have summarized India's past and present and amplified the myriad of historical, cultural, and political facets that exist in this land. Their assignment was to convince 554 states, 542 of which were princely kingdoms whose original treaties with Britain had lapsed, to sign the Instrument of Accession, indicating their willingness to become part of a unified, independent India. On August 15, 1947, only three states stood apart: Junagadh, Hyderabad, and Kashmir.

Less than three months after independence, the Nawab of Junagadh fled to Pakistan with all his belongings, leaving behind a kingdom in chaos and a people who must choose between accession to Pakistan or to India. On February 20, 1948, the people opted for India.

In Hyderabad, a kingdom with its own currency and postal stamps, the Nizam wanted to maintain his royal status and keep Hyderabad as a landlocked, independent country. Attempts to negotiate with the Nizam failed in January 1948. On September 13, 1948, Indian troops entered Hyderabad and peacefully annexed the kingdom.

Jammu and Kashmir, however, were more like chess pieces maneuvered strategically by both Pakistan and India. People of the region were predominantly Muslims. The Maharaja of Kashmir, a Hindu king, negotiated with Pakistan, intending to accede in their direction. Negotiations eventually reached a standstill. In a move to force compliance, Pakistan cut off supply lines to Kashmir. Local unrest ensued. The Maharaja, whose army was unable to contain the tribal fighting, fled from Srinagar, his Kashmiri capital, to Jammu, appealing to India for help. The price for India's military assistance was the Maharaja's signature on the Instrument of Accession. On October 27, 1947, India airlifted troops to Kashmir and extinguished the tribal uprising. Pakistan, who claimed Kashmir because of its Muslim population, would not accept the turn of events.

Well before India's independence from Britain, portions of the subcontinent were colonies attached to other European nations. Goa, a coastal region south of Mumbai, bordering the Arabian Sea, belonged to Portugal. Pondicherry, a region south of Chennai, on the Bay of Bengal, belonged to France. When independence was gained from Britain, the French voluntarily gave up their occupation on the subcontinent. Portugal, however, would not let go of Goa in spite of more than 300 years of revolutions for Goan freedom. To India, the oppression of this small region surrounded by India's own borders opposed the principles that were the foundation of India itself. On December 17, 1961, Indian troops invaded Goa, annexing it almost peacefully in 24 hours. By doing so, India completed the jigsaw puzzle but overrode its own principles of revolution from within by consent of the common people, rather than military conquest.

Becoming independent was one thing; organizing the country and establishing a common infrastructure was quite another. Determining the language of India, for instance, has been a controversy that is still not entirely sorted out. There were fourteen separate spoken languages officially recognized by India's Constitution. In addition, hundreds of dialects language combinations, and local accents existed. A single language was not spoken or understood throughout the country.

One group recognized that English could be introduced as the best-of-all-evils. "English not only prevents our isolation from the world, but also from each other" (Memon & Banerji, p.98). This justification was seen as good by some and bad by others. In addition, most Indians saw English as a foreign language imposed by their oppressors. To adopt English went against India's struggle for independence.

Hindi, the language spoken by a majority of Indian citizens, was also problematic. While it made some sense to adopt Hindi universally, those who did not speak it suspected an underlying motive that would place Hindi speaking communities in a more favorable power position within the country. It was also a point of debate that to select Hindi would lead to the disappearance of individual local cultures, as well as the disappearance of the rich beauty of native tongues and traditions. It would, in essence, eliminate people's roots.

After numerous false starts and considerable bloodshed, most of India eventually adopted a three-language system, including Hindi, English, and the prevalent regional language. The state of Tamil Nadu, however, contending Hindi as historically inferior, has accepted only two languages.

The ripple effects today of multiple official languages seem endless. Schools must teach several languages to each individual, but the combination differs based on location. Learning material, legal ordinances, commercial contracts, and official documents differ according to the language of each state. The language printed in newspapers is often localized. Television broadcasts are not suitable for all people in a single language. One elected official may not be able to communicate easily with another. Script on public signs differ from state to state. Marketing material and technical documentation must be localized. Transportation information must be locally acceptable, but useful to travelers with another tongue. Even today, in addition to English, Indian currency reflects all fourteen of India's constitutional languages.

On January 26, 1950, India's Constituent Assembly adopted a Constitution for Independent India. Drawing on democratic references from around the world, the new constitution formed a parliamentary government with checks and balances built within the representation system and the judiciary system. The Constitution intends to assure equality in a social system built around religious castes. It offers liberty of thought, expression, belief, faith, and worship. It promotes unity of the nation and dignity of the individual.

The challenge of establishing Indian law was particularly difficult. Prior to independence, law in India originated from several sources. Certainly, British law governed some aspects of society on the subcontinent. When it came to local matters, however, the British made a concerted attempt to leave jurisdiction up to the people and their local customs. In most cases, local law was religious law, whether Hindu, Muslim, Christian or some other persuasion. Each persuasion differed considerably in matters related to rights of ownership, family rights, and inheritance. India's first attempt to establish a uniform law in the land was the Hindu Code Bill.

Eventually, the content of this code was separated into four individual acts governing marriage, divorce, adoption, and succession that were passed as a common civil code.

In developing a policy towards foreign affairs, India's independence came at a time of unique global complexity. With cleanup from the Second World War still at hand throughout Europe and Asia, India's leadership adopted a philosophy to "keep away from power politics of groups aligned one against another, which have led to world wars and which may again lead to disasters on an even vaster scale" (Memon & Banerji, p. 51).

As the cold war evolved, few countries were geographically positioned with as great a vulnerability to both China and the USSR as was India. This factor must have made India incredibly interesting to the United States. From India's perspective, the United States' support to Pakistan added the threat of a third superpower to India's borders. In spite of foreign pressure to throw its cards in with each of the large Cold War alliances, India maintained a policy of looking out for her own interests on a case-by-case basis.

By 1961, India's non-alignment attitude evolved globally into the Non-Alignment Movement (NAM), representing in its simplest form a kind of political and national neutralism, and in its broadest perspective a fundamental principle for a national way of life.

During 1959, China began making intimidating challenges to the traditional Chinese/Indian border that was understood to exist in a rugged section of the Himalayan Mountains. Chinese troop buildup in the area and military maneuvers continued until October 1962, when Chinese soldiers advanced into what was considered Indian territory and announced that India was at war with China. India, though ill-prepared for war on this front, maintained a faltering defense in the region for nearly a month, utilizing its own resources. By November 20, 1962, when China's advance appeared to threaten the security of Assam, both the USSR and the USA offered to help India. China, recognizing that India's ability to defend against Chinese aggression was on the verge of changing character, announced a cease-fire on November 21, 1962. Chinese troops retreated to within twenty kilometers of the original Chinese/Indian line of control, annexing a considerable section of what had originally been considered Indian territory, but putting an end to the conflict.

When India's independence was established and the separation from Pakistan conceived, the country of Pakistan was formed as two geographically separate regions—West Pakistan, which is the Pakistan of today, and East Pakistan, which is today Bangladesh. Before long, a civil war erupted within East Pakistan. The Pakistani military, controlled from Karachi in West Pakistan, set about ridding the country of the rebels in the east. As a matter of survival, millions of refugees fled to India. The refugee communities quickly became a haven for discontent and a breeding ground for rebels returning to East Pakistan.

On December 4, 1971, the Pakistani Air Force attacked military air bases in northern India. Before the day was over, the Indian Air Force retaliated by attacking airfields in East and West Pakistan and inflicting fierce damage on the Pakistani Air Force. During the next few days, India set up a blockade in the Bay of Bengal, cut off diplomatic ties with Pakistan, and officially recognized the People's Republic of Bangladesh. In defense of Pakistan, its ally, the USA cut off all military and economic aid to India and sent their Seventh Fleet into the Bay of Bengal. Calling Pakistan the aggressor, the USSR quickly mobilized the Soviet fleet for deployment to the Bay of Bengal.

While this superpower standoff took shape, the Pakistani army found itself caught in East Pakistan with a realistic possibility of being overwhelmed by endless Bangladeshi mobs. After twelve days of war, Lieutenant-General Niazi of Pakistan surrendered unconditionally to his Indian counterpart, and the People's Republic of Bangladesh became an independent country.

While maintaining her position of nonalignment, India, perhaps somewhat by default, developed a military relationship with the USSR. Because of India's ongoing conflict with Pakistan and the USA's support to Pakistan, military defense technology from the USA was not available to India. With India's short Chinese conflict, military defense technology from China was not available to India. The USSR provided India's only option, and the foundation for Indian aerospace and military advancement has evolved based on early generations of military technology that Russia was willing to offer to India.

13

Going Places

"I wish some of folk back home could see the precipice on this side – a grim spectacle most unlike the long gentle snow slopes suggested by the photos."

—George Mallory,
from his diary, June 28,1921

When the time came for a vacation of greater proportion than the one- or two-day weekend outings we had been building into our schedule, we planned an excursion to Goa. An old Portuguese settlement located on India's western coast, Goa was perhaps India's best-known resort region, visited in the tourist season by many Europeans. The drive from Bangalore to Goa could be done in a loop of about 1600 kilometers, with the first-day drive finishing at the coastal city of Mangalore.

We went through a variety of terrains to get from Bangalore to Mangalore. We saw deserts, mountains, forest, jungle, ocean shore, villages, farms, cities and rivers. The mountain range, the Western Ghats, rose from the desert floor to the east with rugged forest-covered slopes. As the road made its way down the western side of the range, it lapped back and forth along the face of a jungle-covered canyon following the

Netravati River. The river was a beautiful wild mountain stream flowing over boulders and waterfalls, often with plush vegetation closing in on its banks.

The road was quite good for a mountain road in India. Two vehicles could squeeze by each other without leaving the pavement and without having to back up. In spite of this, we were amazed to see serious accidents so often on a road that was obviously hazardous. Aside from the normal head-on collisions and rollovers, there was a petrol tanker that a team of people were trying to bring up the vertical wall of the canyon. From the looks of things, the tanker had made a drop straight down to the river. The interesting thing about this project was the device being used to bring the tanker back up. There were two primitive machines. Each was made up of a rough-sawed wooden frame that was anchored to the road with wooden pegs through the frame and into the asphalt surface. The frames were also tied by rope to every rock, bush, and tree close by that had any load-carrying capacity. At the center of the frame, a tree trunk with a half-meter diameter was set vertically so that it could pivot inside the frame. Two holes had been chiseled into the tree trunk perpendicular to each other and long poles were inserted in the holes to turn the trunk with maximum leverage. A cable was fastened to the trunk to form a primitive, home-made winch of gigantic proportions. Imagine retrieving a full-size tanker truck from a cliff with two of these devices. The tanker was plastered with signs warning "Highly Flammable." When we came to this spot, the workers let tension off the cables and waved, with wide grins, as they motioned for us to drive across the rigging.

On the mountainside, we encountered a number of trucks stopped in the left lane along the edge of the road with one or two people laid out on blankets on the pavement at the nose of the trucks. At first we thought

144

these were tragic accidents with bodies waiting to be picked up. In reality, this was the normal place for the truck drivers to have a rest. The drivers parked their trucks in the road as a barricade while they slept on the ground in front of the truck. With a big-enough truck, the arrangement seemed relatively safe.

Once we came out of the mountains, the river became wider and slower. Rural car washes were frequent, where vehicles parked up to their rocker panels in the river water so that the drivers could scrub down the car, truck, auto-rickshaw, water buffalo, or bull. There were spots in the river where groups of people were cleaning laundry by beating the clothes on the rocks and laying them on the grass and bushes to dry. As the river increased to about half a kilometer wide, we saw fishermen out in the current, up to their chests in water, setting out fishing nets. Some of the fishermen were in dugout canoes. Many of the villages we passed had large community water wells with a rough timber spanning the opening and a pulley attached to the timber supporting a rope and wooden bucket.

Mangalore, a stop on the way to Goa from Bangalore, is a port city located on the Arabian Sea. As we drove along the shore of the port, we could see huge cubes of granite, 2 meters by 3 meters by 2 meters, piled up to be exported on ships. There were piles of raw timber, still just tree trunks, that were also ready for export. It was an eight-hour drive from Mangalore to Goa. Much of the drive was on an elevated plateau overlooking the Arabian Sea, similar in many ways to California's shore and rugged chaparral-covered coastal hills. Off the plateau and back at sea level, the terrain was more like Florida's landscape that has been reclaimed from the swamps. These areas were covered with coconut groves and rice paddies.

Goa was originally settled by Portuguese in the 16th century, and many of the names in Goa still had a Portuguese flavor. Goa occupied a moderate size area extending inland on the subcontinent, but Goa's main attraction was its coastline. Charters flew directly to Goa from places like Amsterdam, Paris, and Frankfurt during the tourist season from October until March.

We stayed in a resort located at the south end of Calungute Beach, an eight-kilometer expanse of white, sugary sand. Early in the morning the beach was populated by cattle and local fishermen who muscled in their handmade outrigger fishing boats, dragging in nets with fish, lobsters, shrimp, and anything else their nets may have snagged. Even during the day, when vacationers were out sunning themselves, the beaches were practically empty, with as many local merchants walking from person to person trying to sell silk scarves and other local items as there were tourists.

Early one morning, while I was walking down the resorts steps about to start a jog along the beach, a midsize stray dog emerged from the underbrush and began nipping at my feet. Trying to ignore it, I made for the sand to begin my run. The dog had something else in mind. Before I realized what was happening, the dog had my left leg in its mouth. It wouldn't let go. To stop the beast from biting my leg, I stuck my right arm in his mouth. The dog clung to my arm, not willing to let go of that either. The dog would not let me move forward and also would not let me retreat. I finally dragged the animal back up the steps, latched to my arm until reaching the top step. A hotel security guard was not far away. The guard didn't speak much English. Trying to explain what had happened was futile. We both laughed at the attempts to communicate in sign language.

Meanwhile, another lone jogger ran past the dog and successfully headed down the beach. This made me wonder if I was being picked on. Perhaps what had happened to me was a fluke and the dog may have just gotten overly excited. I decided to do exactly what the other jogger had just done. This time the dog immediately bared it fangs and got a hold on my right leg. I rammed my left arm in its mouth to protect the leg. The security guard broke into a run, coming after the dog with a large stick. After two good whacks, the dog disappeared for good back in the underbrush at the edge of the sand.

My limbs seemed to still be working. Without paying much attention to the attack that had just occurred, I began a long, slow jog down the beach. The cadence of the run took my mind off the dog, and after several hours I had covered the beach from end to end. I walked back to the hotel room. Cathy noticed that my legs and arms were covered with blood. Looking more closely, each limb had bloody slashes crisscrossing the flesh where the dog had grabbed on. Fortunately, no muscle had been torn, but the dog's teeth had managed to slice the skin in numerous spots. I looked like I had lost a fierce fight with a thorn bush—twice.

There was not much question regarding whether I needed to be treated for exposure to rabies. I began a series of seven injections that went on for ninety days. When we left the resort, the authorities were still trying to find the dog. Over the next few weeks, Cathy became adept at giving injections.

Calungute Beach was anchored on its south end by the remains of an old Portuguese fort. Beyond the fort, the shore was made up of steep cliffs with waves that fiercely hammered the rock walls making it nearly impossible to approach the water's edge. This was a great spot for rock climbing, with a variety of skill levels to challenge each of us. We could walk small paths cut into the side of the cliff, climb the jagged boulders near the water, and view the ocean from old remnants of the fort.

147

Nick scaled the exterior of the fort wall. Near the water there were pools in the rocks where water and sea creatures were left by waves and the tide.

Goa's open-air tourist market was impressive. Selvan dropped us at one end of the town's main street and picked us up at the other. The street was lined with vendors selling their wooden, brass, silk, stone, and silver items from blankets spread out on the sidewalk. Behind these vendors were the regular open-front shops, which looked only slightly more permanent than the blankets.

The trip back to Bangalore from Goa was a mad dash. We began early one morning and headed back up through the jungle-covered mountains to the Deccan Plateau. This jungle was dense in spots, with vines hanging from the trees and gigantic ferns at ground level. Trees shot straight up, fighting for light, and towered over the mountainsides. The jungle was so thick that during the day no sunlight could reach earth below. This was wild country, with signs along the way warning of tiger habitation. Reaching the top of the plateau, we were out of the rain forest and back into desert. From the road we could occasionally see the remains of medieval fort walls, kingdoms that are now only legends.

Driving back to Bangalore, we managed to reach a top speed of about 100 kilometers per hour, the fastest we traveled during our entire stay in India. The roadside was littered with the remains of automobile accidents from the previous week. Signs posted along the road indicated how many accidents had occurred in the last year—how many injuries and how many fatalities.

Approaching a village about halfway between Hubli and Bangalore, we began to see the activity of a market for the sale of bulls. The event consumed the entire village, with creamy white, humped-back bulls tied to every small tree. On the way into the village, bulls were being led to town by people on foot. The animals were washed and looking their best. As we drove away from the village, we saw men walking along the road with the bulls they had purchased. We knew some of these individuals would need to walk for at least two or three days before reaching their destination. 100 kilometers per hour suddenly seemed like the speed of light.

One of the most remote business destinations to which I routinely traveled was a town in northern India called Renukoot. There are two things of interest in Renukoot: a hydroelectric dam, featured on India's 100-rupee notes, and an aluminum smelter operated by Hindalco. By any standard, Renukoot was out of the way. At the time, the trip from Bangalore included a flight to Delhi, another from Delhi to Varanasi, and a five-hour drive over a broken highway to Renukoot. The return trip was even less direct, often with a short stop by the airplane in Lucknow on the way to Delhi, and Chennai on the way from Delhi to Bangalore.

Varanasi was a city of note. It was located on the River Ganga in the state of Uttar Pradesh. Its name comes from being situated between the Varuna and Asi tributaries flowing into the most sacred Hindu river. The city's older name was Benaras. Varanasi is reputed to be the oldest living city on the face of the earth. Its origins date back to primitive civilization, and it is still a thriving city today, one of India's ten largest. The Ganga begins in the Himalayan Mountains and makes its way to the Bay of Bengal, negotiating a wide bend at Varanasi on the way. The river flows through the heart of the city. One of India's most photographed scenes could be seen every day along the river in Varanasi as hundreds of Hindus, on their life's pilgrimage, took a spiritual bath in the Ganga.

Varanasi is a hub of Hindu history. As legend has it, when time began, a pillar of light, representing enlightenment, is reported to have broken through the crust of the earth's surface and flared up into the sky at this location. Now Hindus from all over the world make pilgrimages to Varanasi. In addition, many devout Hindus come to Varanasi to die. Because the river is holy, Hindus who can afford cremation have their ashes sprinkled over the River Ganga. All day, every day, there were Hindu funerals in the city. Bodies, wrapped in rags, were transported on top of cars, rickshaws, or other devices to the ghats on the river where they were cremated on individual bonfires and then sent into the water.

Varanasi looked to me like a city of utter chaos. One building stood on top of another, constructed and reconstructed over the centuries. The streets were dark, barely wide enough for people to walk past each other, not nearly wide enough for vehicles. It was an endless maze of ancient passageways and dead-end alleys that provided access to every corner of a human honeycomb. The busy passages were lined with shops, with all the action of a market. Outside of the stone city, where the streets were a bit wider, hundreds of bicycle rickshaws with bamboo canopies transported everything from school children to freshly made bricks. Varanasi was known for its hand-woven silk cloth made in small dark rooms on looms constructed of roughly-sawed wood. It was some of the finest silk work in the world, often laced with threads of gold to accent the distinctive designs and colors.

Coincidentally, Sarnath, the birthplace of Buddhism, was only twelve kilometers from Varanasi. An ancient stupa stood at Sarnath where a tablet was found with inscriptions that predate any other Buddhist writing. It was at Sarnath that the Buddha preached his first sermon, and Buddhism flourished there for more than 1,000 years.

When leaving Varanasi for Renukoot, we hired a driver with an old Ambassador to bring us the distance. The road leaving town was blocked for traffic in our direction. Several police officers were stationed at the intersection to be sure that vehicles didn't enter the one-way route from the wrong direction. Our Ambassador driver stopped next to the police officer and described his predicament.

"This man is from America and must go to Hindalco at Renukoot. We must be permitted to drive this way down the road in order to reach our destination in time."

I didn't quite understand the logic of the driver's argument, but with a stern nod from the senior officer, we drove against traffic for nearly eight kilometers. Traveling north from the city was like leaving the last outpost of civilization. It was upon leaving Varanasi that I saw my first caravan of camels.

A new highway was being put in along the road to Renukoot. Bits and pieces were complete. The finished sections were some of the best stretches of road I had seen in India. The other segments were some of the worst. This all resulted in an average speed of only about fifty kilometers per hour. Had we driven faster, the Ambassador we were in might have self-destructed. The drive started with a long stretch that twisted through desert terrain. There were small villages along the way that had tiny, doorless clay homes with thatched roofs and dirt floors. Many of these villages were without electricity. Water was available only from the village well, a large open shaft that a wooden bucket could be lowered into. The air temperature was intense, hitting 47 degrees centigrade during the day. It is not uncommon for the temperature to exceed fifty degrees centigrade in this region during the hottest part of the summer.

Eventually the road climbed into a rugged, hilly, forested area. Renukoot was in this hill country, less than one day's drive from the border with Nepal. What was Renukoot like in 1996? Well, progress had made its mark in the last thirty years. There was money (not much), roads (sort of), electricity (in places), a major aluminum smelter (certainly), an Indian hotel with a restaurant (six tables), a public telephone, and, well—hmm—some goats, a tailor, a pile of old tires, a shed with a side of mutton hanging from the rafters, a couple of chickens, and, of course, the ever-present cows. People walked along the roadside with wooden yokes supported over their shoulders, carrying their load from place to place.

An individual who had helped to build the original aluminum plant in the early 1960s described the location as being so remote at that time that currency had little meaning. The entire local economy was based on barter. One of the challenges in setting up the plant in the beginning was to convince the local residents of the benefit of currency.

Business travel frequently brought me to Pune, a city similar in many ways to Bangalore and located on the western side of the country. On my second trip, the Holiday Inn had been my home for four days and the stay had been trouble-free. When checking out, I was thinking what a great place this hotel had been and gave them excellent marks on their quality survey.

"What time should I be in the lobby to catch the shuttle to the airport?" I asked the desk attendant.

"A shuttle will get you to the terminal twenty minutes before the flight. It is plenty of time sir."

The attendant confirmed a time and made arrangements to call me out of the hotel restaurant when the shuttle was scheduled to depart. I was getting a bit restless after ordering a meal because time was getting late, and the food had not arrived yet. I hurried things along a bit and managed to finish up with a few minutes to spare. The lobby attendant saw me coming.

"I will be in the lobby rather than the restaurant when the airport shuttle arrives."

His expression instantly turned to a look of panic. "You are going to the airport?"

The attendant dashed out of the hotel front door just in time to see the shuttle car turning the corner on its outbound trip. He had evidently sent the shuttle away ten minutes early with another guest who he thought was me. This caused the hotel lobby to turn into a situation of utter chaos with the concierge and desk attendant finding out what could be done, the hotel manager scolding the concierge, and—in the midst of this—someone trying to get another car arranged. All this happened just when things had been going so well for me at the hotel. The concierge asked me to sit down and relax. The lobby staff continued to argue among themselves and argue on the telephone. To be honest, I considered hitchhiking as an option to get to the airport on time.

As the clock ticked, the situation was reaching the point of no return with less than half an hour until my flight departure. I told the concierge that the car they were arranging might get me to the airport, but if it took much longer, I would end up at the airport with no plane. He made a few calls. Within another five minutes a car and driver came racing to the front door. The concierge said a few words to the driver as I threw my bags into the trunk. The driver seemed excited. The horn was honking before he left the driveway—without a single obstacle in sight. This was where the fun began. By some strange coincidence, the roads were almost empty of traffic, making a clear shot to the airport. I think the driver went as quickly as was reasonable, perhaps eighty kilometers per hour, while he laid on the horn every three or four seconds. The driver was just doing this for effect to emphasize that he was trying hard. As we raced down the streets, we were drawing all the attention of a presidential motorcade. It was an interesting ride and must have been a crazy sight for all the people on the sidelines. I made my flight, running from the car to check in and directly onto the airplane.

It was January when we visited Calcutta on the way to Nepal for a short holiday. Calcutta was a city with many of India's modern features located on the mouth of a branch of the River Ganga. It was crowded, notably busy, dirty in spots, and certainly disorganized.

During our stay we had the good fortune to stay at Tolleygunge, a private club that was an indigo plantation during the 1700s. It was also a spot where Tipu Sultan stayed in exile for some time while being chased by the British in the early 1800s. Cathy and the children spent two days sightseeing. They rode in a small wooden boat on the river, visited the Victoria Memorial, and spent an afternoon at Science City.

I joined a colleague and took care of two days of business. We traveled through narrow passageways of the city, encountering obstacle after obstacle. At times we reversed our vehicle for a full block to allow larger vehicles or a truck to pass. Bicycles, pedestrians, and rickshaws moved chaotically through congested alleys. After more than two hours in this traffic maze, we turned a final corner and arrived at the factory we intended to visit, located in a decrepit complex in an old corner of the city.

The compound was surrounded by a brick wall. Several buildings made up the factory. Its forge, which we had come to see, was actually outdoors with only a sheet-metal roof protecting it from the weather. The forge stood on raw ground without a footing under its base. Piles of small, forged components lay on the earth around the machine. Two thin men, using a crude tong, reached into the furnace nearby and pulled out red-hot pieces of steel to place into the die for the hammer to form. With each thump of the hammer, the forge shook, the ground shook, and the men at the machine shook.

An engineer led me into an old building attached to the factory to an office with a state-of-the-art computer graphics terminal and a modern electro-deposition machine for making the forge dies—yet another example of Indian contrast. The facility was able to transfer information electronically for the design and production of dies as well as produce dies automatically. Yet the dies, once manufactured, were inserted into a 1910-style forge hammer which was merely sitting on the ground, outside, in the middle of loose piles of parts, and operated by a man in sandals.

When the time came to leave Calcutta, we sat in the airport looking out the window at a beautiful day, but our flight was delayed for five hours because of fog in Kathmandu. We waited patiently. Our plane eventually took off and flew across India's northern border before descending through clear weather over the Himalayan peaks into Nepal's largest valley.

I commented to the woman at the arrivals gate, "It must have been quite foggy here. Our flight was delayed for half a day."

"No sir," she confidently replied, "The flight was delayed because of fog in Calcutta."

Interesting.

Although I had made many business trips to Delhi, when we arrived as a family, we were coming from Nepal, entering at the international airport. As with any international entry, our first checkpoint after leaving the plane was the immigration desk. Stepping up to the counter, I handed the immigration attendant our paperwork. The officer looked at me, looked down at the passports, and looked over his glasses at me in a suspicious kind of way. I thought that we were in for a real going over by the Indian authorities. The man called for his supervisor and then ushered us to another desk.

We had no idea what was going on. Soon all the immigration officials had left their stations and were looking over the person processing our paperwork. The man was struggling. He looked at us, looked at the passports, looked at the immigration forms, and, without a smile, whispered to his supervisor.

Our concern mounted. We knew how tough it could be to correct a problem at immigration. As more people gathered, we were wondering what was amiss. While passengers began to back up in the arrivals hall, the group of immigrations workers continued to fiddle with our documents, whispering to each other from time to time and pointing at the computer terminal. After nearly forty-five minutes, with annoyed travelers filling every queue, the supervisor looked up and smiled. With a final thump of the entry stamp, the attendant handed the passports to the supervisor.

The supervisor reached over the desk with an outstretched arm returning the documents and explained, "You are the first passengers we are processing with our automatic passport scanner. The scanner saves time and reduces the size of our queues. Thank you for your cooperation."

Looking back at the crowd behind us in the arrivals hall, I chuckled and replied, "I think it is doing a very good job of that."

The supervisor laughed and shook my hand.

We spent a day in Delhi processing paperwork at the Chinese embassy for visas for our return trip. As a reward for our patience, we decided to hunt down the newly opened Delhi McDonald's. It had been nearly a year since we had eaten at a fast-food restaurant. This one, India's first, had only been operational for six months. There were already plans for five more in the city. The menu was indigenous, offering lamb-burgers rather than hamburgers, with the premium feature, the Maharaja Mac, a close cousin to the Big Mac. All six of us loaded up on burgers, fries, and soft drinks like we had found an oasis in the desert. The manager saw the enjoyment we were all having and came to ask if there was anything more we would like. A glance around the table got an affirmative nod from everyone.

"I think we need one more round of exactly what we just had, please."

She looked startled. "One more round!" A pleased grin appeared on her face. "Okay, sir. One more round!"

Delhi is the political center of India. It houses India's main embassy district, a clean, well-organized, parklike setting. Other sections of the city, with resources including impressive government buildings, elegant hotels and convention centers, and upscale restaurants and shopping districts, set Delhi apart from most of India. Still, much of the city is congested, with air pollution so bad at times that visibility is significantly affected. I was in Delhi for one business trip when power and telephones were out city-wide for more than three days. On another trip I was stranded in the city for three days because all flights to southern India were vastly overbooked. The waiting lists were longer than 200 people per flight. To return to Bangalore, I was finally able to get a confirmed flight to Chennai after three days, and from Chennai, traveled over land for eight hours to reach Bangalore. Today many of Delhi's worst infrastructure problems have been significantly improved.

14

India Today
Snapshots of Daily Life
Updated in 2023 by Lakshmi Srinivas

"But since we operated a protected environment till 1991, none of India's industries were truly internationally competitive. Costs were high, quality low and technology obsolete. In industry there is only one guru who teaches you to be efficient and that is not business school but a buzzword called competition. Without competition, industry will not be competitive and if not competitive, we will perish – leave alone prosper."

—Rahul Bajaj, 1997,
from *India 50: The Making of a Nation.*

Ram, a mechanical engineer living in Pune and working as a purchasing agent for a construction company, visited Bengaluru for three days of business. Early the first morning, Ram called an old friend from school.

"Shyam, has your family made plans for tomorrow evening yet? Can we meet for dinner?"

Ram arrived early at the small restaurant on Lavelle Road. He wanted to be sure a table was available. At the entrance to the restaurant, Ram noticed a string of fresh green chilies with a lemon attached below hanging down from the center of the door. Not being from Bengaluru, Ram wondered what this was. He stopped the restaurant manager.

"I haven't seen that before," Ram said, pointing at the string hanging from the door as the manager walked by the table. "What is it for?

"We keep that in the door to ward off evil," the manager politely replied with a smile.

Ram thought it was a good idea.

Many Indians today are highly educated, living with advanced technology integrated into their daily lives, and are somewhat superstitious. Today, India is a combination of the age-old ritualistic practices, rationality, and modernity. The peculiarity of India lies in the fact that ancient practices coexist with the latest developments of the world. In main urban areas, the world's latest scientific trends are either produced locally or are almost immediately introduced as imports. At the same time, age-old practices continue to be a way of life in rural areas.

Vastu, the ancient Indian practice dictating guidelines for positioning and constructing houses and businesses, has strict followers in modern India. Factors related to *vastu* are said to influence the success of a business, health and safety in a home, and a variety of other aspects of life. It is not uncommon for buildings that have been constructed with unfavorable *vastu* to be demolished in India.

Politicians and ministers today frequently consult with swamijis while making major decisions related to the government, the political party, and their personal lives. Swamijis are religious and cult leaders who each have their own set of followers. Political negotiations are often achieved through the swamijis.

Astrology is as much a part of Indian life today as it was centuries ago. For example, in many parts of Tamil Nadu, it is common to see a man sitting on the pavement with a cage containing two parrots. He spreads out cards face down on a cloth at his side. When a client squats in front of the astrologer, the man chants and lets one of the parrots out of the cage. The parrot looks at the client, picks up a card, and brings it to the astrologer who interprets its meaning. Today's India presents a multidimensional culture in which modern life does not replace ancient practices: they co-exist.

Ram thought back to several decades ago when he could shop for his daily needs and pay cash. He remembered staring at a worn-out Rs.100 note that the shopkeeper returned as part of his change. He faced many situations where ragged currency notes received in one shop were not accepted by another, making it difficult for Ram to spend the money in his wallet before his next visit to the bank to exchange worn-out notes. He thought of the small denomination currency he routinely needed to carry around—notes and coins. Daily life included acquiring, carrying, handling, and exchanging currency. Life seems easier today. Now Ram simply uses a smartphone to scan vendor payment QR codes for all his daily transactions—restaurants, stores, small shops, and even street vendors. No cash is required. Many of his common household needs are purchased using his mobile phone with app-based shopping. Ram remembers that it was not so long ago when he stood in long queues waiting for his spot at the teller's window to manage his banking needs. Now he uses a mobile phone and internet banking.

As a middle class has emerged in India with income levels increasing across all segments of society, many new things, which they had not imagined in years gone by, have become available and affordable to Indians. Embracing technology-driven infrastructure, Indians of all income levels have transformed to a digital lifestyle.

Ravi, a bank employee in his mid-40s, wakes up one morning and thinks back to his college days. Ravi remembers stepping into the street to flag down an autorickshaw that would take him to where he needed to go. Frequently, finding an autorickshaw willing to bring him to his destination was a time-consuming effort.

Ramya, Ravi's daughter, begins the day chatting on her mobile phone with her classmate, Vinita, about preparation for the medical school entrance exam. Vinita, whose goal is also to become a doctor, tells Ramya that she is not so worried about entrance exam preparation because she has heard that medical school entrance requirements overseas are much easier than what is required in India these days. Yet, Ramya is determined to attend an Indian medical school. She knows that her studies for the entrance exam will be difficult, but she is confident about the quality of education she will receive in India.

Ravi knows that Ramya will take an autorickshaw to school today. She will book it using a smartphone app. An autorickshaw will arrive within five minutes of her booking. With GPS-enabled transportation facilities for app-based autorickshaws and taxis, Ravi worries less about Ramya's ability to secure her daily transportation than he did when he was attending college.

Despite India's constitutional declaration of equality, elements of the traditional caste system continue to be cultural factors that are slow to change in Hindus' lives. Rekha and Tanuj, belonging to different Hindu communities, were colleagues at work and decided to marry. Their families were enraged when the duo announced their decision and went so far as to break ties with the couple. For many Indians grounded by custom, any threat to tradition is not easily accepted. As an increasing number of professional marriage-age young men and women interact closely in the workplace, the percentage of Indians who forego the traditional parental arranged marriage and select their own spouse, is also increasing.

Rekha and Tanuj, as a working couple, now have two teenage children and live on the outskirts of Bengaluru. Together, they try to build in a good work-life balance. Rekha, like many women in her situation, tends to her family's needs alongside her career. She enjoys the sunrise while sipping coffee on the balcony of their 15th floor apartment complex. As she leaves the apartment for her office, she takes a long walk to her car in the underground carpark. Rekha returns home to freshen up and heads to the apartment clubhouse for a workout in the gym after a taxing day at work. In a daily, ritual-like pattern, she meets several of her neighbors there. Tanuj and the children each have their own social lives within the apartment complex, each with many friends in their own age groups. As neighbors, the residents all gather as a community to observe festivals that happen throughout the year.

"Why don't we plan a family trip to Mumbai in October?" Rekha suggests to Tanuj. "This time we can drive."

"Well, that would be an adventure," Tanuj replies. "I hear that with the new highway network, it is less than a 17-hour trip. We can do it."

Tanuj thinks back to when they vacationed in Mumbai six years ago. The train journey had taken 24 hours. At that time, an overland drive to Mumbai would have been considered impractical for a short vacation. Though they have never driven to Mumbai before, Tanuj is not worried about uncertainty of the route. They will follow safe, multi-lane highways, allowing their smartphone GPS app to be their guide.

Vacationing travelers of India's middle class today can also select from several low-cost airlines that fly to many locations inside the country. This has brought long-distance holiday travel in India within reach for many Indian families who only two decades ago were unable to consider such possibilities. When travelers arrive, the metropolitan areas of more than a dozen Indian cities are now equipped with metro-trains for their local transportation while also providing a comfortable, affordable city commute for city residents.

Shashi, a forty-year-old Hyderabad resident, heard the cry of Sarita, her elderly mother. Sarita lay immobile on the bathroom floor, her hip bone fractured from an unexpected fall. Shashi, using her mobile phone, immediately called for an ambulance. On the road, the congestion of traffic parted with cars, trucks, motor scooters, and bull carts merging left to allow a narrow opening for ambulance passage. Less than one hour after her fall, Sarita was admitted to a nearby private hospital. A team of doctors, including the orthopedic surgeon who attended to Sarita, scheduled her surgery to be within 24 hours. The surgery was successful.

Shashi considered her good fortune. It was not so long ago when families had to wait hours for an ambulance to reach their homes. Calling the ambulance had its own complexities with landlines only sporadically available within communities. If an ambulance arrived, it began a precarious journey to get to the hospital, often caught in world-class traffic snarls. If patients survived the journey, they began an endless wait for a doctor's review and diagnosis before treatment could begin. Today, Indian healthcare and pharmaceutical medicines are more accessible, higher quality, and more affordable than they were when Shashi was small.

India's history and customs form a timeless foundation for its culture. As infrastructure, technologies, wealth, products, brands, habits, and ideas continuously change in India, they meld into a contrasting mixture in the present, blending old and new, past and future. It is a colorful combination of tradition and possibility that is played out in the daily lives of every Indian.

15

The Mosquito

"Nobody knows the exact incidence of malaria in India, for village vital statistics are, perforce, kept by primitive village watchmen who put down to 'fever' all deaths not due to snakebite, cholera, plague, a broken head, or a few other things they recognize. But a million deaths a year from malaria may be regarded as a conservative estimate of India's loss by that malady."

—Katherine Mayo, 1927,
from *Mother India*

Coming from Michigan, we were quite familiar with the mosquito. I have even heard it called Michigan's state bird. India is blessed with a slightly smaller and vastly more lethal variety. Before departing for India, we visited the travel clinic at a hospital in Detroit. The consultant there reviewed the locations through which we expected to travel, compared it to cases of disease in those areas, and promptly inoculated us for everything against which we needed protection.

One risk that was published for India was malaria, particularly the chloroquine-resistant strain. This meant that to get the maximum protection available, we needed to take what was, at the time, the latest generation of antimalaria medication—a once-a-week mefloquine pill. To use this medicine properly, one needed to begin taking it three weeks before entering an area at risk and continue for three weeks after leaving.

We all began taking the medicine in May, while still in the USA, and continued for more than fifty doses, until after our first trip back to the USA. My body began to rebel just before our first return. One afternoon I felt nauseous. Actually, it was something a bit more than being dizzy. I thought I might have been drugged. I lay on my bed to relax and felt as if my body was floating off the mattress. This went away after half a day, and I didn't quite know what to attribute it to.

When we returned to the USA, I had sustained a low-grade dizzy spell. I chalked it up to jet lag and ignored it. After more than two weeks of not feeling up to speed, I began to wonder whether the problem was more serious. I was taking two medications, Rabipur and mefloquine. The packaging on each warned against symptoms exactly like those I was having. I could not discontinue the rabies vaccination. I stopped taking the mefloquine. For several days I still sensed that something was not right and finally went to the clinic. Unfortunately, no one knew exactly what to make of the symptoms. The symptoms were not so specific, and I seemed to be getting better on my own. When it was time to return to India, the travel clinic felt it was important for me to continue taking the Lariam. I struck a compromise and agreed to only take the drug if I went to areas where malaria was more of a problem than in Bangalore.

No sooner did we arrive back in Bangalore than I needed to travel to Renukoot. I took the weekly dose of mefloquine again. After the fourth week I had a spell that left me lying in bed the whole day feeling like my body was floating again. I discontinued the pills and felt pretty good for about three weeks. Then one morning I went for my normal morning run, pushed off to work feeling great, and by noon, in desperation, called Pammi to help me home. I was too weak to stand on my own. Pammi supported me as we made our way to the flat. I laid on my bed in a kind of half-sleeping trance for three days, feeling like the world championship racquetball tournament was being played in my head. The inside of my skull was the court. Cathy stayed by the bedside and held my hand. I couldn't eat. I was utterly exhausted. It seemed difficult to breath, yet when I paid close attention, my breathing was fine. I could hear and feel every heartbeat in my head. Sometimes I thought that my heart was accelerating out of control, and at other times, I thought like it was beating only a few times each minute. Cathy verified that the heart rate was normal. I felt like I was running a fever and my body was shivering—my temperature was normal.

After several days I began to nurse myself back to the real world, forcing food and water into my system and getting out of bed for a few minutes every day. It was more than a week after the spell began that I felt well enough to visit a doctor at the Baptist Hospital to help me understand the problem a bit better. I slowly shuffled into the waiting room with Cathy's shoulder supporting me. The doctor had seen this before. He called it mefloquine toxicity, a reaction in the nervous system to the anti-malaria medication. He told me what the problem was called and told me the only thing I could do was to wait for the poison to get out of my system. I plotted a kind of half-life for the doses I had taken and determined that I should begin to feel better by about the middle of August.

After ten days I began to get short breaks from the dizziness and pounding in my head. Each day I improved slightly. After two weeks the floating sensation would only stay for a few hours each day. The jackhammer pounding against the inside of my skull went on almost continuously for three weeks.

I entirely missed ten days of work, then began visiting the office for only a few hours at a time. I had good days and bad days. Every time I began to feel healthy again, another spell would hit that lasted several days. By late August the spells were getting shorter and less severe. I trained myself to tolerate the spells a bit more, knowing that they would pass if I rested. I knew I could continue the normal activities of the day. By the end of August, I had returned to full days at work.

We searched the internet and found a site dedicated to anecdotal accounts written by people who had similar experiences as a result of taking mefloquine. Many of them were in such out-of-the-way places in Africa and Asia that their conditions were compounded when misdiagnosed as malaria or typhoid by rural doctors, and then treated for a nonexistent ailment. Many reported suffering from severe depression for up to a year, a side effect that I was fortunate to avoid. My favorite quote from the internet stories was: "Malaria is hell. Mefloquine is hell. Make your choice." How true.

16

2003 Epilogue
Going Home

"Oh, Danny, Danny! We've had this rare streak o'
luck. Let's quit winners for once. Cut and run while
the running's good."

—Michael Hardwick's novel "*The Man Who Would Be King*"
Based on Rudyard Kipling's "*The Man Who Would Be King*"

Five years have elapsed since we left India and
journeyed back to Michigan. I have returned to Bangalore
several times each year since then, watching from the
sidelines as change has enveloped the country. On each
trip I have been astonished by advancement that has
surfaced in one arena or another. To those living the
change, what is happening must be almost imperceptible.
One by one, roads in the city have been divided in the
center with granite barriers, keeping traffic on each side
of the road moving in only one direction. Traffic signals
are appearing at intersections, and many drivers are
cooperating with the signals. A fly-over has been
completed at the city market, giving vehicles a fast path
over congested areas in the center of the city. When it
was first completed, Selvan and I made a special detour
just to drive the fly-over from end to end.

Many of the roads in Bangalore were resurfaced
using an automatic blacktop machine that laid an entire

lane at one time. The lane separation lines were still applied manually. A team of painters and supervisors worked in the center of the road while traffic passed on either side. Rocks were placed along the work area to discourage vehicles from crossing the freshly-painted dash marks. At one end of the group, a supervisor laid out each dash individually with a tape measure and straight edge. The supervisor was followed by a number of barefoot painters, each with a small pail of high-gloss yellow enamel and a brush. The painters squatted on the balls of their feet as they each applied fresh yellow paint in the rectangular dash the supervisor had drawn on the black surface.

One year ago, I arrived in Bangalore and stepped off the airplane onto a carpeted jetway leading to the terminal. I thought back to when we had returned to Michigan and stepped off the plane at Detroit Metropolitan Airport onto a similar carpeted jetway. I had gotten on my knees and kissed the ground, just as I had warned the children I would.

Looking out one of the Bangalore terminal windows, I could see a Lufthansa Boeing 747 parked in the freight bay. It dwarfed any other plane that I had seen in Bangalore and reminded me of the time during our stay when a commercial 747 had accidentally landed at the military airport near Chennai rather than at the commercial airport a number of kilometers away. This caused numerous problems. Not only were civilians deposited squarely in the center of a restricted area without normal facilities to remove them, the runway itself was too short for a normal takeoff of a 747. The plane's interior had to be stripped clean to reduce its weight. After sitting near the end of the runway for more than a week, one of India's best military pilots successfully revved up its engines and launched the bird into the air, landing it safely at the commercial airport close by, where it was reassembled.

Heineken beer was on the menu at the Oberoi on my last trip to Bangalore. There was a choice of six imported beers, but I found myself ordering the local Kingfisher just for old times' sake. The Pizza Hut that had become a weekly treat for the family had become one of a number of Pizza Huts in Bangalore. The staff we had known during our stay was dispersed to the various startups around town, and a new batch of employees looked after the original restaurant. In Bangalore, the original Pizza Hut, with its imported menu and ingredients, as well as its New York decor, was listed as a five-star restaurant. Now Domino's, its American competitor, and the Pizza Corner are scattered across town.

When it came time for us to depart from Bangalore, we left behind two years of our life, perhaps the most rewarding two years we had known. I thought back to the life of my father's father and knew that we had connected with his existence for a short time. We had seen some things he had seen, things that left mainstream America long ago. We had felt some things that he had felt, knowing that our lives depended in small part on our own resourcefulness and in large part on the grace of God. Each morning we woke up not knowing what we would encounter, but certain that, if we were going to accomplish what we needed to that day, we would have to find a resourceful way to navigate around unexpected obstacles.

After returning to Michigan, a number of Indian colleagues from Bangalore have had the opportunity to travel to the USA for short periods of business. With wide-eyed reactions similar to ours when we first arrived in India, they have greeted each day with surprise and amazement. The routine things that we take for granted have made the greatest impression. The free flow of traffic on an interstate highway, the size and scope of a large department store, the variety of box cereals on the shelf at a local supermarket, dishwashers, automatic car washes, a house without a security fence, a frozen lake, a leafless tree in the spring standing next to a colorful evergreen; these have caught their attention.

Seeing their reactions has made me understand that we are much the same—human beings, thriving in our own environments, looking curiously at those who have grown up elsewhere. Each comes from an environment filled with good and bad, rich and poor, tolerant and unforgiving. We each admire the resourcefulness of the other. We are both best off when we can chuckle at our own shortcomings when placed in the other's setting. For each it is good to see what the other has done, but there is no place like home.

The day finally came when Cathy and I followed the children for the last time up the portable stairs positioned next to the wing of a small Air India jet parked on the runway at the Bangalore Airport. We took our seats in two rows near the center of the plane. I looked out the window one more time to see the flowering trees dropping their petals to the ground and the rows of palms bent over in the breeze.

"Excuse me, sir, would you like a refreshment?" A neatly dressed flight attendant carrying a tray of sweet lime juice and Thums Up shifted the tray in our direction. I looked up from the drinks to see the attendant's name tag. Ravi—I should have known.

The plane was about to taxi from its parking spot when I noticed a small green lizard staring up at me curiously from the pavement below.

"Goodbye, my friend."

Resources and References

Alexander in India. (n.d.). Retrieved July 4, 2003. http://wso.williams.edu/~junterek/india.html.

Aryabhata (476-499). (n.d.). Retrieved July 4, 2003. http://www.math.sfu.ca/histmath/India/5thCenturyAD/Aryabhata.html.

Baht, M. & Murthy, U.R.A. (1997). *Karnataka.* Bangalore, India : Gangarams Publications Private Limited.

Blake, S. (1993). *Shahjahanabad: The Sovereign City in Mughal India 1639-1739.* Cambridge, England: Cambridge University Press.

Dickinson, M. B. (1990). *National Geographic Picture Atlas of Our World.* Washington, D.C.: National Geographic Society.

Durant, W. & Durant, A. (1967). *The Story of Civilization: Part X—Rousseau and Revolution.* New York: Simon and Schuster.

Habib, I. (1997). *Akbar and His India,* New Delhi, India: Oxford University Press.

Hodges, W. (1793), *Travels in India During the Years 1780, 1781, 1782, 1783.* London, England: J. Edwards.

Judd, D. (1972). *The British Raj.* East Sussex, England: Wayland Publishers Ltd.

Kakar, S. (1981). *The Inner World.* New Delhi, India: Oxford University Press.

Keay, J. (1987). *Banaras: City of Shiva.* New Delhi, India: Brijbasi Printers Private Limited.

Longhurst, A. H. (1996). *Hampi Ruins Described and Illustrated.* New Delhi, India: Asia Educational Services.

Mayo, K. (1927). *Mother India.* New York: Harcourt, Brace & Company.

McCridle, J. W. (1960). *Ancient India as Described by Megasthanes and Arrian.* Calcutta, India: Chukervertty, Chatterjee & Co.

Memon, A. & Banerji, R. (1997). *India 50: The Making of a Nation.* Bombay, India: Book Quest Publishers.

Miller, H. (1969). *Wild Elephant Roundup in India.* National Geographic, Vol. 135, No. 3.

Nehru, J. (1941). *Toward Freedom: The Autobiography of Jawaharlal Nehru.* New York: The John Day Company.

O'Connor, J. J., & Robertson E. F. (2000). *Aryabhata the Elder.* Retrieved July 4, 2003, from School of Mathematics and Statistics University of St. Andrews, Scotland, website. http//www-groups.dcs.st-and ac.uk/~history/Mathematicians/Aryabhata I.html.

Ottenheimer Publishers, Inc. (1993). *Pictorial Atlas of the World.* Godalming, Surrey, England: CLB Publishing.

Papanek, J. L. (1994). *Ancient India: Land of Mystery.* Alexandria, VA: Time-Life Books.

Phalakska (1986). *History of India (Beginning to 1536).* Tiptur, India: Shashi Prakashana.

Srinivasachar, S. (1995). *Hampi, The Fabled Capital of the Vijayanagara Empire.* Mysore, India: Directorate of Archaeology and Museums.

Thurston, E. (1992) *History of the Coinage of the Territories of the East India Company in the Indian Peninsula and Catalogue of the Coins in the Madras Museum.* New Delhi, India: J. Jetley for Asian Educational Services.

ALSO AVAILABLE

Paperback and eBook

Turning Ten
Great Adventures in the Great Lakes
2nd Edition

Be inspired by the true story of four outdoor adventures made by ten-year-old children in the Great Lakes region with their father.

Now 30 years after the first Turning Ten adventure, this 2nd Edition includes reflections about the lasting legacy of these four trips.

The adventures include backpacking the full-length backbone of Isle Royale; canoeing the Au Sable River from its beginning as a small stream near Frederic, Michigan, until it empties into Lake Huron; riding a tandem bicycle from near Ann Arbor to Mackinac Island; and completing an 80-mile journey through Lake Huron's North Channel in a tandem sea kayak.

ALSO AVAILABLE
Hardcover

Building The Bunkee
A Photo Anthology of
Custom Log Cabin Construction
and
One Man's Retirement Dream

With a series of photos and brief descriptions, Dan Ellens shows step-by-step how to hand-build and furnish a high-quality, off-grid log cabin using many supplies provided by the land. This charming cabin has everything needed for tranquil, electricity-free life in the wilds.

Building the Bunkee also shows how to construct a luxury rural outhouse, a sturdy firewood shed, and how to build the various tools and fixtures that Dan used to helped him work alone and safely in the woods.